HARDPRESS.NET
HOME OF HARD-TO-FIND BOOKS

Edmund Burke
by John Morley

Address:
HardPress
8345 NW 66TH ST #2561
MIAMI FL 33166-2626
USA
Email: info@hardpress.net

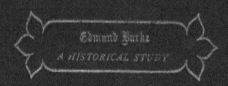

Edmund Burke

A HISTORICAL STUDY

EDMUND BURKE:

A HISTORICAL STUDY.

EDMUND BURKE:

A HISTORICAL STUDY.

BY JOHN MORLEY,

B.A. OXON.

London:

MACMILLAN AND CO.

1867.

LONDON:
R. CLAY, SON, AND TAYLOR, PRINTERS,
BREAD STREET HILL.

PREFACE.

A PORTION of the following chapters has already appeared in the " Fortnightly Review." This portion has since undergone many considerable modifications, while the rest, including the whole of the last two chapters, is now published for the first time.

It scarcely requires to be said that the stand-point of my book is not in any sense biographical. When the outward facts of a statesman's life have once been established and set forth in an accessible record, it seems a work of supererogation to ask the reader once more to tread ground with which he is already sufficiently familiar. Mr. Macknight's industry has found out for us all that we can hope to know as to the personal events and dates of Burke's career. From the historical side the case is different. The opinions we hold about every prominent statesman will from time to time need revision, as our view shifts about the events in which he took a part, about the general nature of progress, and about the meaning of all history.

Biography, in the hands of a man of the requisite capacity and sensibility, is perhaps the very highest form of prose work. One may, I think, almost count upon one's fingers the really good biographies in English literature ; but then, alas ! it is not every man whose life would suffice to inspire work of this high and rare kind. The biographer, stripping his subject, as much as he can, of what is irrelevant and accidental in the surrounding conditions, delights the reader with a fresh and impressive picture of a human character. The writer of a historical study, on the other hand, taking much lower ground, aims not at a reproduction of the central figure of his meditations, but at a criticism of his hero's relations, and contributions to the main transactions of his time. This at least is the design of the following pages.

EDMUND BURKE.

Born at Dublin . . . . *January* 12 (N.S.), 1729

Came to England 1750

Went to Ireland as Private Secretary to Single-
speech Hamilton 1761

Private Secretary to Lord Rockingham 1765

Elected for Wendover, one of Lord Verney's
Boroughs. . . . . *December,* 1765

Elected for Bristol . . . . *November,* 1774

Declining the Poll at Bristol, elected for Malton,
Lord Rockingham's Borough 1780

Paymaster-General in the Second Rockingham
Ministry . . . . *April* to *July,* 1782

Held the same office in the Coalition Ministry . *April* to *Dec.* 1783

Retired from Parliament . . . . *July,* 1794

Lost his Son 1794

Died at Beaconsfield . . . . *July* 9, 1797

CONTENTS.

CHAPTER I.

CHARACTERISTICS.

CHAPTER II.

ISSUES OF THE TIME.

CHAPTER III.

THE CONSTITUTION.

CHAPTER IV.

AMERICAN INDEPENDENCE.

CHAPTER V.

ECONOMICAL REFORM, IRELAND, AND INDIA.

CHAPTER VI.

THE FRENCH REVOLUTION.

EDMUND BURKE: A HISTORICAL STUDY.

CHAPTER I.

CHARACTERISTICS.

IT is almost exactly one hundred years since Burke first took his seat in the House of Commons, and it is something like three-quarters of a century since his voice ceased to be heard there on great public questions. Since his death, as during his life, opinion as to the place to which he is entitled among the eminent men of his country has touched every extreme. Tories have extolled him as the saviour of Europe. Whigs have detested him as the destroyer of his party. One undiscriminating panegyrist calls him "the most profound and comprehensive of political philosophers that has yet existed in the world." Another and more distinguished writer insists that he is "a resplendent and far-seeing rhetorician rather

B

than a deep and subtle thinker." A third tells us that his works " cannot be too much your study if you mean either to understand or to maintain against its various enemies, open and concealed, designing and mistaken, the singular constitution of this fortunate island." A fourth, on the contrary, declares that it would be hard to find a single leading principle or prevailing sentiment in one half of these works to which something extremely adverse cannot be found in the other half. A fifth calls him " one of the greatest men, and, Bacon alone excepted, the greatest thinker who ever devoted himself to the practice of English politics ; " and yet, oddly enough, the author of this fifth verdict will have it that this great man and great thinker was actually out of his mind when he composed those pieces for which he has been most generally admired and revered.

These diversities of opinion are not difficult to be accounted for, and they are very well worth considering, both because they are useful in illustrating the general position of English politics in the latter half of the eighteenth century, and because they bear with much force upon the probable course of English political opinion in the latter half of the nineteenth century.

A hundred years ago the government of England had come to a dead lock. For seventy years the Whigs had ruled the country. The Revolution of 1688 was the consummation of that struggle between the sovereign and the nobles which had gone on in England since its conquest by the Normans. The same struggle was universal in Western Europe. It was an inevitable consequence of the decay of the feudal system, after the aim which gave life to it, the defence of the West against the barbarian from the North and the Ottoman from the East, had been satisfactorily accomplished. But the ease of England was peculiar. At the moment when William I. established the authority of the Crown, the nucleus of a strong coalition against it already existed in the partially dispossessed and exasperated Saxon nobles. For one of its effects, this accelerated the contest, and the English nobles assailed the authority of the Crown before the corresponding but inverse movement began in France,—where the Crown had to attack the authority of the great nobles. Another effect was, that in England the people, sympathising with the Saxon originators of the coalition, and identifying the Crown with all that they had to detest in Norman oppression, uniformly sided with the nobles against the

Crown. This attitude became traditional, and receiving a fresh impulse from the assumption of an unpopular religious supremacy by the monarch, survived the defection of the nobles to their former rival in the Great Rebellion. This kind of defection has been a common characteristic of the history of Western Europe during the break-up of the mediæval system. In France, for example, the monarch having first crushed the nobles by the help of the people, afterwards patronised them, and struck an alliance with them against the people. In England, the nobles in the same spirit felt instinctively that the Crown, which they had reduced to a position of safe inferiority to themselves, was to be supported against the people, their own ally in earlier times. This did not, however, prevent them from again courting the popular support, when they supposed that James II. was about once more to assert the authority of the monarchy. Their alarm, which was perhaps justified by the strength of the reaction they had done their best to promote thirty years before, probably made them sincere in their proclamation of free and popular ideas. A few nobles adhered to the principles which had been learnt in the Civil Wars, and stuck to the Crown. But the majority understood the interests of their order more correctly, and their sagacity had been rewarded with prolonged power.

But now time had robbed them of the little handful of tolerably disinterested chiefs who had once led them, as well as of the tolerably disinterested principles which the party had so long found it convenient to profess. The inevitable exposure which must sooner or later come upon every oligarchy overtook the oligarchy of the revolution families. The patrician senators forgot to continue to hold on the popular mask, and the bugbear of Jacobitism had at length fallen fairly to pieces. The Divine Right of Kings had been fully expanded into the Divine Right of Nobles. The nation saw a select horde of peers wrangling for places and for the public money, devoted to selfish and low-minded intrigues, and perfectly indifferent to the welfare of the State. There was no more in this than the invariable issue of an oligarchic system under all conditions and in all countries. Time and security soon wear off the thin whitewash which distinguishes a patrician Whig from an avowed Tory. Every system of government which rests upon the capacity of a very small and charily recruited body, is sure in time to become a monstrous burden to the community in which it prevails, and to find itself confronted with popular revolution in a more or less violent form.

There were two quarters from which the corrupt Whigs of a hundred or a hundred and ten years ago might have expected the decisive attack to be made— the Monarch and the Commonalty. The first vigorous-minded ruler who should come to the throne was sure to despise their incapacity and resent their patronage. The first breath of political life and agitation that should stir the people would instantly disclose the selfishness and incompetency of their protectors. As it happened, they offended the conceit and self-will of that ignorant youth who in 1760 ascended the throne of Great Britain. The struggle which began thus ignobly between the uneducated and obstinate youth and the oligarchs who thwarted him for their own ends, lasted until the former had grown into an uneducated and obstinate adult, and most of his original opponents had ceased to live. The old Whig party was broken up in 1770. Chatham and the Rockinghams were thoroughly estranged and disunited. George Grenville's death had left a certain strong section of Whigs free to enlist under any banner. Another and more powerful section were deprived of a leader by the death of the Duke of Bedford. Lord North's ministry was strengthened by recruits or renegades from both of these connexions ; by the Earl of Suffolk, for example, from the Grenville section, and by the Earl of Sandwich from the Bedford section. The Duke of Grafton also was restored in 1771, on the death of Halifax.[1] But this transformation of the North government was in a manner a partially accidental and temporary absorption of the old families. The Tory principle that the king should not be obliged to take a minister who should be displeasing to him, as against the old Whig principle that the king was the doge of an oligarchic council, was not precisely established until 1783. The contest between George III. and the old Whigs was over in this year, when the King, having by a sort of sly, dull, underhand imitation of a *coup d' état,* sent down Lord Temple to menace the House of Lords with his displeasure in case they passed Fox's India Bill, got the Bill thrown out. With his usual rude impetuosity, he sent the next day to demand the seals from the Coalition cabinet. The question at issue in this twenty years' war had been the right of the sovereign to choose his own ministers. The King won. He had kept Lord North in power for twelve years. He turned out the Coalition,

---

[1] *Stanhope,* v. 293. *Massey,* ii. 70. Donne's *Correspondence of George III. with Lord North,* i. 48, *seq.*

he installed Pitt. The sway of the revolution families was finally broken ; their exclusive title to place and pay finally abrogated.[1] This much was at least settled, that the monarch, whatever else he might be, should at all events not be a puppet in the hands of Whig chieftains ; and that the government of the country, to whomsoever it might fall, should no longer be the appanage of a band of incompetent nobles, whose only claim to it was that their grandfathers had dethroned a king by whom their pride had been wounded, and by whom the Anglican clergy, his rivals in bigotry, had been irritated and alarmed into revolt against their own ecclesiastical principles. "The general election of 1784," Lord Russell says, "determined for more than forty years the question of the government of England."

[1] In 1782 Fox prophesied to Pitt under the gallery that the Rockinghams would go out, and the old system be revived. "And they look to you," he added. "If they reckon upon me," Pitt replied, "they may find themselves mistaken." Fox afterwards repeated this, and said, "I believe they do reckon on Pitt, and I believe they will not be mistaken." Sir G. C. Lewis says that "neither of the parties in this dialogue were quite right in their anticipations" (*Administrations of Great Britain from* 1783 *to* 1830, p. 76), and argues that the contest between Fox and the King ended in a compromise. He does not mean, I take it, that there was any compromise on that part of the contest which turned on the King's independence of the old connexions in choosing his minister. This feature at least of the old system was distinctly revived and sustained.

Meanwhile, events had happened which had made the King's victory of 1783 far less decisive in his own favour than it might have seemed to him and to others at the time. It was a final victory over the Old Whigs, but it inflicted no more than a momentary defeat on the New. This party, which performed so conspicuous a function in English politics, and the lingering remnants of which still figure on the political stage, was the creation of Edmund Burke. Most of them vilipended him bitterly in later days. Some of their political descendants vilipend him now. With the usual insolent thanklessness shown by patricians in every age and country towards the greater plebeians who supply them with ideas and a policy, the party never offered him a seat in their cabinets. But for all that, he was their inspirer. To him they owed the whole vitality of their creed, the whole coherence of their principles, the whole of that enlightenment, that rational love of liberty, that antipathy to arbitrary ideas, on which rest their just claims to the gratitude of their descendants. Burke, from 1770 to 1790, was in the politics of the eighteenth century what Wesley was in its religion. He entered into the midst of the valley and found it full of dry bones. By his imagination, his reasoning, his enormous knowledge, above all, by his ardour and impetuosity of character, he brought the dead Whig principles up from out of the grave, and kindled a life in them, which has only just flickered out for ever in our own days. He made a vigorous effort to restore popular ideas to that high place in practical politics from which they had been excluded ever since the glorious days of the Great Rebellion. From the Restoration to the Revolution, the spirit of reaction enjoyed a scarcely disturbed triumph. From the Revolution down to the accession of George III. English statesmen were all absorbed either in maintaining or overthrowing that final movement for aristocratic supremacy, of which in truth no more than the mere prologue had been completed with the dethronement of James II. There was no room for ideas until the task of suppressing Jacobitism had been brought to a decisive close; and even when this was done, and the ceaseless intrigues and machinations of fifty years were thoroughly and for ever baffled, time was still needed in which the statesmen of the old school might gradually disappear to make way for others, who to a new set of circumstances should bring a new set of maxims and a new spirit. It was Burke who first seized the true significance of the situation, who first proclaimed the principles of the rising movement, and who thus led the Whigs to the forgotten truth, that a government exists for the sake of the whole people.

Bolingbroke, abandoning the old theory of Divine Right, had seen this as clearly as either Burke or any other thinker. The whole argument of the *Patriot King* turns on the doctrine that the good of the people is the ultimate and true end of government. Locke himself furnished this base to Bolingbroke's famous speculation, " That since men were directed by nature to form societies, because they cannot by their natures subsist without them, nor in a state of individuality, and since they were directed in like manner to establish governments, because societies cannot be maintained without them, nor subsist in a state of anarchy, the ultimate end of all governments is the good of the people, for whose sake they were made, and without whose consent they would not have been made." [1] Starting from this, Bolingbroke expounded the spirit in which a patriotic monarch would govern his subjects, insisting that he should make no difference between his own rights and those of his people, except in regarding the first as *trusts,* and the last as absolute *property.* If George III. trained as he is said to have been in the doctrines of this work, had possessed capacity and

[1] *The Idea of a Patriot King,* p. 118 (ed. 1749).

generosity enough to understand and assimilate them, if he had even distantly resembled his illustrious cousin, the King of Prussia, the history of this country might have moved in a very different direction from that which it has actually taken. But instead of being a hero, George III. was only a dull man with a rather bad heart. He did not understand his own principles, and even if he had had ability enough to understand them, he had no ability to carry them into practice. There is nothing more fatal, either in private life or in the larger affairs of state, than for an incompetent man to grasp a principle of action that is too big for him. Such was the case with this wretched sovereign. He tried to play the good despot over the vast empire of Britain, with a capacity barely above the mark of a parish constable. Within ten years he brought England to the verge of revolution. Within twenty years he had dismembered the empire.

It was necessary therefore to start afresh from the familiar and established basis on which Bolingbroke had constructed his ideal system. If Frederick II. of Prussia showed the possible advantages which it contained, George III. of England proved its certain and unavoidable perils still more unmistakeably. Burke's *Thoughts on the Cause of the Present Discontents*, written when George III. had been ten years upon the throne, is the virtual refutation of the *Patriot King*. Events had already shown the idea to be pregnant with unspoken mischief, unless you can always be quite sure that your patriot king will be great enough and strong enough for his post. Burke understood the true significance of these events. Their lesson impressed him profoundly. He saw that the government of all by one had broken down very evidently, and very disastrously. He concluded that the only remedy was to return to " the ancient lines of the constitution," to the system of the government of all by a virtuous and public-spirited few, who would be the reflection of the wishes and interests of all. He did not rise to the still higher conception of a government of all by all, of a whole people by themselves. Prussian autocracy, or its boorish imitation at St. James's, filled him with apprehension and hatred. But I am unable to find any evidence throughout his writings that he had a glimpse of the true opposite of the system of Bolingbroke, of which our modern type, the great Western Republic, has risen to grandeur since Burke's death. Burke's theory was fundamentally and in ultimate principle not very different from Bolingbroke's. There are two ways of viewing government.

According to one, all government should be for the people; according to the other, it should be not only for the people, but by the people. Burke was as far as Bolingbroke from admitting the latter of these two conflicting theories. He saw that the government by a bad and narrow-minded sovereign, assisted by a contemptible clique, was not government for the people in any sense. An aristocracy with popular sympathies seemed to him then, as it always did, the true remedy for the revolutionary feeling which was at that time so dangerously visible, as well as the best embodiment of true and permanent principles of government. The House of Commons was then a highly aristocratic body. Burke admired it on this very account. The House of Commons was designed as "a control for the people." Never at any time did he abandon this tutelary view of the relations between the people and the House; that the legislators chosen by a few electors were to be humane, wise, far-seeing, animated solely by consideration for the welfare of all those for whom they legislated. Yet what is this but the theory of the good despot in another shape and with a new face?

Before examining this more fully, let us return to the historic side, and notice once more that to Burke the revival of the Whig party was due. His eloquence and ardour acted on them like the touch of the spear of Ithuriel. They flung off the degraded shape which had grown about them, and sprang up with new fire and new vitality. The chief of modern Whigs has extolled the service rendered to the country by Burke's *Thoughts on the Present Discontents*, " by instilling into the minds of young politicians, who at that time were greatly increasing in number throughout the country, those wise and beneficial principles which their Whig ancestors had practised, but which the old intriguers of that day had entirely forgotten." To realize the difference between an old Whig and a new Whig— a Whig of 1760, and a Whig of 1780—we may study the conduct of a great chief of Earl Russell's own house, two years before the publication of that book which was the signal for the revival of the party. " In 1768," says a historian, himself a Whig, " instead of taking a course worthy of his name and ability, the head of the house of Russell was intent only on securing the preponderance of his own weight in the government. What that government should be was a secondary object. His first desire was that it should be constituted principally of his nominees. The Court might take what line of policy they pleased ; the Whigs might be a scattered and disbanded corps ; the

Duke of Bedford would not take the responsibility of office upon himself; but must have his Gowers, his Weymouths, and his Rigbys in administration."[1] This is what Whig principles had come to, and must always come to in the long run, as well as all other principles which erect either a privileged governing class or a single privileged ruler. The corruption of Bolingbroke's theory in so pitiful an imitation of a Patriot King as the Third George, was not worse or more injurious to the common weal than the corruption of the Aristocratic theory in so pitiful an imitation of an "aristocratic body with popular sympathies" as the Duke of Bedford and his crew. If we would learn the impulse which Burke gave to this corrupt and fallen faction, we have only to compare the Duke of Bedford, as Mr. Massey has described him, with such men as Charles James Fox, and Windham, and Grey, and, greatest of them all, with Burke himself.

There may, perhaps, be said to have been four leading movements of political thought in England in the eighteenth century. The first was initiated by the Whigs of the Revolution, and proceeded on the assumption that a benevolent Providence created the

[1] Massey's *History of England during the Reign of George III* i. 366 (ed. 1865).

people of England in order that they might be governed by a select number of patrician families. With the second, we may associate the names of Bolingbroke, who expounded it with unrivalled brilliance and force, and of Bute, North, and George III., whose signal incapacity brought it in the course of twenty years to an ignoble and contumelious end. The third movement was initiated by Burke, and carried on by disciples who went further than their master. The fourth movement rose at the end of the American War of Independence, received a powerful impetus from the ever memorable outbreak against feudalism and privilege in France, was checked again by the horror which some of the excesses of that outbreak aroused, was forcibly repressed during that most dismal period in English history from 1794 to 1815, burst forth again uncontrollably after the peace, wrung the Reform Bill from the patrician oligarchy, wrung new poor laws and free trade from selfish or ignorant squires, and will, before long, still further impair that fabric of artificial privileges which must deservedly fall when they have become dissociated from the notion of superior political obligations.

It is very unjust to Burke to overlook the great services which he rendered by promoting one of these movements, because he failed to grasp the spirit of the greater movement which followed it. Why do men so habitually choose to fasten upon what their most eminent benefactors failed to accomplish, when they might instead find so much to admire, to revere, and to be eternally grateful for, in what they actually achieved?

Let us remember the debasement into which popular principles had come a hundred years ago, and the revival which took place immediately after Burke took up the study and practice of politics. Let us remember all the noble schemes which he originated or furthered, the enlightened methods which he brought into politics, the unshaken hostility with which he opposed all arbitrary principles and all arbitrary measures, the indomitable industry and perseverance with which he brought a great state criminal to judgment. Let us remember, in fine, how many of the wise measures which it has been reserved for a happier time to carry into full effect, were advocated and anticipated by him.[1]　Those

[1] To illustrate this, I cannot do better than quote Mr. Buckle's list of the bad measures which Burke assailed, and the good measures which he defended. "Not only did he attack the absurd laws against forestalling and regrating, but by advocating the freedom of trade he struck at the root of all similar prohibitions. He supported those just claims of the Catholics which, during his lifetime, were obstinately refused, but which were conceded, many years after his death, as the only means of preserving the integrity of the empire.

are guilty of the sin of injustice to the past who consent to ignore all these achievements, because Burke's principles stopped short of the point to which some of the party that he had himself created afterwards insisted on dragging him. Those, on the other hand, who, because Burke was wise and great in his generation, declare that in his writings we have the best possible guide to the true foundations of " the singular constitution of this

He supported the petition of the Dissenters that they might be relieved from the restrictions to which, for the benefit of the Church of England, they were subjected. He opposed the cruel laws against insolvents by which, in the time of George III. our Statute-book was still defaced ; and he vainly attempted to soften the penal code, the increasing severity of which was one of the worst features of that bad reign. He wished to abolish the old plan of enlisting soldiers for life—a barbarous and impolitic practice, as the English legislature began to perceive several years later. He attacked the slave trade, which, being an ancient usage, the king wished to preserve, as part of the British Constitution. He refuted, but owing to the prejudices of the age was unable to subvert, the dangerous power exercised by the judges, who, in criminal prosecutions for libel, confined the jury to the mere question of publication, thus taking the real issue into their own hands. And, what many will think not the least of his merits, he was the first in that long line of financial reformers to whom we are deeply indebted. Notwithstanding the difficulties thrown in his way, he carried through Parliament a series of bills, by which several useless places were entirely abolished, and, in the single office of Paymaster-General, a saving effected to the country of 25,000*l.* a year."—*History of Civilization*, vol. i. pp. 420—422. There are one or two drawbacks to all this, as will be shown in the text in the proper place.

fortunate island," are guilty of the still worse offence of impeding present progress and future well-being.

The question whether Burke was not a rhetorician rather than a thinker, does not appear to deserve any very elaborate discussion. The simplest solution is also the true one. He was both a rhetorician and a thinker. He had a profound power of examining the relations among political ideas in the light of political practice, and he constructed from them a complete and coherent system of his own, which, indeed, to men who live in a later age may seem to rise from shallow and uncertain foundations, but which, for all that, rested on a consistent theory, and was the starting-point of a new and a very important movement in advance of the then existing habits of thought among statesmen. It is surely impossible to deny the title of a thinker to one who perceived, as Burke did, the profound speculative truth that politics is not a science of abstract ideas, but an empirical art, with morality for its standard; or who mastered so thoroughly, as Burke did, the great doctrine that " nothing universal can be rationally affirmed on any moral or any political subject." There is scarcely any political writer whose speculations contain more valuable truth on this point than those of Burke. " The lines of morality," he says in one place, "are not like ideal lines of mathematics. They are broad and deep as well as long. They admit of exceptions ; they demand modifications. These exceptions and modifications are made, not by the process of logic, but by the rules of prudence. Prudence is not only first in rank of the virtues, political and moral, but she is the director, the regulator, the standard of them all."[1] And again, in the famous speech on American taxation, he implores the House to revert to their old principles. He scorns the argument that England had a right to tax her colonies, as such an argument deserved to be scorned. " I am not here going into the distinctions of rights," he cries, " not attempting to mark their boundaries. I do not enter into these metaphysical distinctions. *I hate the very sound of them.*" Again, "This is the true touchstone of all theories which regard man and the affairs of men— does it suit his nature in general?—does it suit his nature as modified by his habits?" In another place, " As no moral questions are ever abstract questions, this, before I judge upon any abstract proposition, must be embodied in circumstances ; for, since things are right and wrong, morally speaking, only by their rela-

[1] *Appeal from the New to the Old Whigs*, vol. i. p. 498, *a*, of Burke's Works (by H. Rogers, 2 vols. 1842).

tion and connexion with other things, this very question of what it is politically right to grant depends upon this relation to its effects. It is the direct office of wisdom to look to the consequences of the acts we do." [1] " The excellence of mathematics and metaphysics is to have but one thing before you ; but he forms the best judgment in all moral disquisitions who has the greatest number and variety of considerations in one view before him, and can take them in with the best possible consideration of the middle results of all."

This, it should be borne in mind by those who impugn the unity of Burke's earlier and later views, was spoken years before the French Revolution had brought metaphysical abstractions and the distinctions of rights into such tremendous prominence. It is not by any means certain that all of those who either deny or maintain Burke's right to a place among powerful thinkers have even now realized and accepted this profound lesson, that in politics we are concerned not with barren rights, but with duties ; not with abstract truth,

---

[1] Burke's Works, i. 172, *b* ; ii. 488 ; *Speech on the Petition of the Unitarians,* Works, ii. 478 ; *Speech on Bill for Shortening Duration of Parliaments,* Works, ii. 482, *a.* In truth there is no end to the passages of this kind that the student may collect from Burke's works. In scarcely a single piece do we miss at least one expression of aversion to abstractions. Cf. especially the *Speech on Conciliation with America,* Works, i. 200, *b* ; 183, *b.*

but with practical morality. Yet what more indisputable law, what more important principle, has ever been contributed to the stock of political ideas ? If this method had occupied the place in the minds of politicians to which its profound value entitles it, the volume of history would be without two of its most fatal chapters. It would lack, first, the record of those fatuous struggles, to enforce a right only because it is a right ; and second, the still more painful chronicle of those great men who have wasted lives of noble purpose, lofty ideas, heroic endurance, in endeavours to carry out beneficent schemes in the face of an iron antagonism of circumstance and conditions. If Burke's contemporaries had all understood as thoroughly as he did the fruitlessness alike of abstract rights and abstract ideals, we should not have had to read the history of our war with the American colonies, nor the history of the failure of such men as Joseph II. and Charles III.

It has been reserved for a great thinker of a later day to explain the source and significance of absolute conceptions in social subjects, and to insist on the substitution of relative ideas in their place. This is the natural result of the substitution of the Positive for the Abstractional philosophy, inasmuch as the latter proposes to study the nature of Beings, while the former only studies the laws of Phenomena and supposes a gradual improvement of observation. We may now comprehend the absurdity, on scientific grounds, of setting up absolute and immutable types of government. We have now been at least partially instructed in the hopelessness of supposing that "social phenomena can be modified at will," "that the human race has no spontaneous impulsion, but is always ready to yield to any influence of the legislator, spiritual or temporal, provided he is invested with a sufficient authority." [1] Burke, though he was not in a position to place this doctrine on the inexpugnable scientific basis which belongs to it, and on which Comte has placed it, was still directed to it by virtue of his native vigour and acuteness. We shall consider this further when we come to the epoch of the French Revolution, and the consummation of those metaphysical and absolute ideas which Burke so vehemently rejected.

If Burke had achieved nothing else beyond the discovery (for it was a discovery with him) and enforcement of this great truth, he would clearly have established a position in the front rank of political thinkers. But this, and the much more that he did in

---

[1] Cf. Comte's *Positive Philosophy*; Miss Martineau's Translation ii. 72.

the same department of thought, has been partially overshadowed by the qualities which made him a rhetorician as well as a thinker. His natural ardour always impelled him to clothe his conclusions in glowing and exaggerated phrases. Nobody would be disposed to deny that Bentham was a thinker, and yet he constantly displays a heat, an acrimony, a contemptuousness, that is only different from the unphilosophic language of Burke in being less majestic and overwhelming. A rhetorician deals with words and images, and, hurried by them out of the path that leads to truth, is thus in the long run deprived even of a desire to find it. Burke's style unquestionably partook of that *opimum quoddam et tanquam adipatæ orationis genus* which the Roman orator has described. The framework of what he has to say is too thickly overlaid with Asiatic ornament. His language burns with too consuming a blaze for the whole to diffuse that clear, undisturbed light which we are accustomed to find in men who have trained themselves to balance ideas, to weigh mutually opposed speculations, in short, to argue and to reason with no passion stronger than an intense desire to discover on what side or on what sort of middle way the truth lies. Those who have acquired a love for political thought amid the almost mathematical closeness and precision of Hobbes, the philosophic calm of Locke, or even the majestic and solemn fervour of Milton, are in a manner revolted by the unrestrained passion and the decorated style of Burke. His passion appears hopelessly fatal to anything like success in the pursuit of Truth, who does not reveal herself to followers thus inflamed. His ornate style does not appear less fatal to that cautious and precise method of statement, suitable to matter which is not known at all unless it is known distinctly.

To understand this more clearly, we must constantly remember that Burke was actively engaged in the thick of the political fight. This was a source both of weakness and of strength to him. It weakened him as a philosopher, because he came to the consideration of his problems with something of a sinister interest in solving them in one way rather than another. If he could find a solution that was in accordance with Whig tactics, or what was still narrower, but still better for himself, a solution that justified the Rockingham section of the Whigs, it was to his interest to do so— not his interest in any sordid sense, for Burke's character was not of a kind to yield to or even to be conscious of temptations of that order, but to his interest as a keen partisan whose peace of mind was staked in the fact of his party being in the right. We shall have occasion further on to discuss Burke's own views as to the uses and obligations of party. There can be no question that his passion did constantly blind him to those loftier considerations which should always be present to the mind of the philosopher, and that in one portion of his career (1788-9) he actually surrendered himself to a systematic factiousness that fell little short of being downright unscrupulous. At the same time it is just to remember that the most memorable act of Burke's public life was his unhesitating abandonment and violent disruption of his party when what he conceived to be the dictates of political wisdom were no longer the guide of their conduct. He was never so obstinately deaf to the voice of what he took for wisdom, never so utterly given over to intellectual reprobation, as to regard allegiance to his associates as the prime and most binding of all duties. He frequently voted away from his leaders and friends. He had barely been in the House a year before he declined to vote for a motion brought forward by Dowdeswell, and supported with all their might by the Rockingham and the Grenville sections of his party, proposing to take a shilling in the pound off the land-tax :—a motion which was carried against the Government, the very spirited country gentlemen in that day, as in later times, caring more for their pockets than even for their party.[1]   He always stedfastly opposed that motion which Fox had ever so much at heart, for the repeal of the Marriage Act.   It is true that Burke quitted the Whigs with circumstances of as much passion as he had been wont to show in his adherence to them.   Still the mere fact that towards the close of a tolerably long career he should have kept his mind sufficiently open to perceive, and his honesty sufficiently vigorous to cleave to, the new and barely suspected deductions from his principles which the French Revolution forced upon him, is worth taking into account when we hear that Burke had too much of the unflinching party-man about him to be a true thinker.

Although Burke's position as an active member of a party thus tended to unfit him for fertile speculation, on another side it gave him peculiar strength, and both by the direction into which it turned his inquiries, and the tone which it imparted to his treatment of them, largely contributed to his remarkable influence on the men of

---

[1] "It is plain," Lord Chesterfield wrote to his son, "that all the landed gentlemen bribed themselves with this shilling in the pound." Cf. *Earl Stanhope's History*, v. 177.   For another example of Burke rising superior to partisanship, cf. *Adolphus*, iv. 210.

his own generation, and still more upon those who have followed him. Burke's speculations always had reference to a practical problem. They were not conceived by a student in his closet; but by a member of the Legislature in the middle of the political arena. A narrow Utopianism—the besetting weakness of most other great writers on politics—was impossible with a man situated as Burke was situated. This inevitably straitened the range of his ideas. But it gave them an air of substance and solidity which served to attract the sympathy and admiration of men to whom bare general ideas were not less detestable than they were to Burke himself. It is a characteristic of the English mind—and it was stronger a hundred years ago than it is now—that we hardly know how to reconcile ourselves to accept more than one general principle at a time, and then it must be exhibited in its practical application to a special case then and there before us.

Like a Roman jurisconsult, Burke gave responses upon individual sets of circumstances. It was the merit of the jurisconsult—in Mr. Maine's words—that "he viewed each case as an illustration of a great principle, or an exemplification of a broad rule." Burke's merit was of a similar kind. He did his best in what he wrote, if not in all that he spoke in the

House of Commons, to trace out the general ideas, the greater principles, which lay at the bottom of the political events of his time. He did this not so much for the sake of the general principle, which was the object of the jurisconsult, as to gain a deeper knowledge of the special fact or set of circumstances. It was with these that he was concerned. " Circumstances," he says, never weary of laying down his great notion of political method, " give, in reality, to every political principle its distinguishing colour and discriminating effect. The circumstances are what render every civil and political scheme beneficial or obnoxious to mankind." [1] This was, perhaps, the only guise in which his hearers in the House of Commons could have been persuaded to accept the existence of such things as general principles at all.

Apart from any systematic political speculation, it is difficult to name another publicist whose writings are so thickly studded with those unsystematic products of an acute, enlarged, and reflective mind, which are vaguely labelled as Wisdom. Burke's mind was so vigorous, his acquired knowledge so large, and his opportunities of observation so wide, that the accumulation of this kind of wisdom in his pages, and the addition which he made

[1] Works, i. 384, *a*.

to the human stock of so valuable a possession, appear no more than a natural result. In his wildest moment these sagacious apophthegms were present, green places in a wilderness of declamation. Many of them have got imbedded in the current phraseology, and men use Burke's maxims without knowing who is their teacher. His pages, as we turn them over, are bright with these luminous utterances. " People will not look forward to posterity, who never look backward to their ancestors." " Crimes are the acts of individuals, and not of denominations." " He that accuses all mankind of corruption ought to remember that he is sure to convict only one." " Angry friendship is often as bad as calm enmity." " The rights of men in government are their advantages." " I have constantly observed that the generality of people are fifty years at least behindhand in their politics. There are but very few who are capable of comparing and digesting what passes before their eyes at different times and occasions, so as to form the whole into a distinct system. But in books everything is settled for them, without the exertion of any considerable diligence or sagacity. For which reason men are wise with but little reflection, and good with little self-denial in the business of all times except their own. We are very uncorrupt and tolerably enlightened judges of the transactions of past ages. . . . Few are the partisans of departed tyranny; and to be a Whig on the business of a hundred years ago is very consistent with every advantage of present servility. This retrospective wisdom and historical patriotism are things of wonderful convenience. . . . I believe there was no professed admirer of Henry VIII among the instruments of the last King James; nor in the court of Henry VIII. was there, I daresay, to be found a single advocate for the favourites of Richard II." Wherever we turn, we are sure to come upon similarly shrewd observation and wise monitions, the instructive results of the close contact of a bright and powerful mind with a wide variety of men and affairs.

Burke did not escape from the peril that was inherent in his own method, and which was largely increased by the atmosphere in which his life was passed. We are too familiar in our own days with the supercilious air with which the practical man—of whom the average member of the House of Commons is the most conspicuous type — turns from inquiries that seem to tend to the modification of existing beliefs. This practical man cannot understand why anybody should think it worth while to disturb the mental comfort of the most sluggish of his contemporaries, or to throw all society into agitation and confusion, merely for the sake of showing that Moses, for example, was not the author of the Pentateuch, or that there are discrepancies in the Evangelists' accounts of a given transaction, or that the voice of science gives forth oracles that do not harmonize with the voice of revelation. Such a class is a heavy burden on the mind of a country. They may stimulate and irritate some in the pursuit of a kind of truth, which is not capable of being quoted like bank stock, but they discourage more. They cannot sympathise ever so remotely with that temper which seeks truth for its own sake, apart from its consequences, and apart from its agreement or disagreement with reigning convictions. This is the natural tendency of men concerned exclusively with practical affairs; and even Burke's powerful intellect did not escape it. For instance, he always expressed the utmost contempt for those writers who are summarily classed in modern phrase as the Eighteenth Century Deists. It was not merely that he felt pain at their conclusions, nor dislike of their method. That they should have ventured into this particular ground at all, fretted him and filled him with uncontrollable

D

anger. Talking of the "philosophic cabal" in the
Reflections, he asks, "It is not with you, composed
of those men, is it? whom the vulgar, in their blunt,
homely style, commonly call atheists and infidels? If
it be, I admit that we too have had writers of that
description, who made some noise in their day. At
present they repose in everlasting oblivion. Who,
born within the last forty years, has read one word
of Collins and Toland and Tindal? and that whole
race who call themselves Freethinkers? Who now
reads Bolingbroke? Who ever read him through?"[1]
This may remind us very strikingly in its tone and
substance of an eminent statesman's contemptuous
refutation of the doctrines of a batch of heretical
books, by the statement that they were all stolen
from Germany. As if the fact either that a doctrine
had first been promulgated in Germany, or that people
no longer read the book in which it appeared, were a
conclusive proof of its falsity and hollowness. Nothing
can be more unworthy, more intensely and shamefully
disrespectful to truth, than to fall back as Burke
does upon the vulgar and their blunt and homely
style. As if the vulgar would not, in their blunt
and homely style, call everybody an atheist and an

---

[1] Works, i. 414, *b.*

infidel, and any number of other ugly names, who should venture to hold opinions that fall outside the limits of their own unexamined traditions; and as if the questions which these men raised could be settled by a simple appeal to the sale of their books. " Ask the London booksellers," cried Burke, " what is become of all these lights of the world." Just as if, because a book had run its course and accomplished its task, therefore it must have been a bad book, and the questions which it opened must have been closed again, and left on their old footing. Do we say that the subsistence which supported bodily strength twenty years ago, or last week, must be pronounced bad and a failure because it is no more to be seen ? Do we call a cannon-ball a failure, because, after its force is spent, it lies rusting and inert on the field ?

Burke's abhorrence and contempt of the philosophic cabal was not, as is often said, the result of the Revolution. Among the host of distinct passages in his writings, or in his conduct, which show that Burke's later history is no more than the development of the principles of his early history, and not separated, as Mr. Buckle, Lord Brougham, and so many others maintain, by a deep chasm—the work of age, toil, disappointment, and the anguish of his beloved son's

death — let me not forget to point out that only
three years after the publication of his *Thoughts on
the Present Discontents,* and seventeen years before
the composition of the ever-memorable *Reflections,*
he denounced the philosophers with a fervour and a
vehemence which he never after surpassed. He had
just returned from France, where he had been brought
into contact with some of the conspicuous Freethinkers
of that momentous epoch. He had occasion to speak
in favour of a Bill for the Relief of Protestant Dissenters, and he made it an opportunity for denouncing
all those whom, somewhat after the blunt and homely
style of the vulgar, he summarily classified as Atheists.
" Have as many sorts of religion as you find in your
country, there is a reasonable worship in them all," he
said ; " the others, the infidels, are outlaws of the
constitution—not of this country, but of the human
race. *They are never, never to be supported, never to be
tolerated."* " These," again he says, " are the wicked
dissenters you ought to fear ; these are the people
against whom you ought to aim the shafts of law ;
these are the men to whom, *arrayed in all the terrors
of government,* I would say, ' You shall not degrade us
into brutes ;' these men, these factious men, are the
just objects of vengeance, not the conscientious Dis-

senter; these men who would take away whatever ennobles the rank or consoles the misfortunes of human nature, by breaking off that connexion of observances, of affections, of hopes and fears which bind us to the Divinity, and constitute the glorious and distinguishing prerogative of humanity—that of being a religious creature; against these I would have the laws rise in all their majesty of terrors to fulminate such vain and impious wretches, and to awe them into impotence by the only dread they can fear or believe, to learn that awful lesson, *Discite justitiam moniti, et non temnere divos.*"[1] This tremendous onslaught on people who ventured to use their understandings, and arrived at conclusions which did not happen to be those of Burke himself, shows that he had, even in his earlier days—for this was spoken in 1773—not gone much further into the true grounds and propriety of toleration than ecclesiastical dignitaries in our own day.[2]

A year before this Burke had in the same way assumed an attitude identical with that of the least liberal and enlightened people among ourselves. A hundred years ago there was the same ferment about Subscription to the Thirty-nine Articles as prevails at

[1] Works, ii. 473.
[2] See *Appeal from New to Old Whigs*, Works, i. 502, *a.*

this moment. After an agitation which had lasted about five years, a petition was at length presented to Parliament in 1772, signed by two hundred clergymen, and about forty members of the professions of physic and civil law. The petitioners " represented the subscription as injurious to the Christian religion by precluding inquiry into the true sense of Scripture ; by enabling unbelievers to reproach the clergy with prevarication and flexibility to objects of lucre or political consideration ; by affording to Papists the advantage of reflecting on the religious establishment as inconsistently framed ; by dividing the clergy, and by occasioning scruples and embarrassment of conscience to thoughtful and worthy persons in regard to entrance into the ministry, or cheerful continuance in the exercise of it." And, still more curiously illustrating the view then current of religion as a thing existing only for the sake of being proved, " the clerical part of the petitioners complained of being obliged to join issue with the adversaries of Revelation, by supposing the true sense of Revelation to be expressed in the established system of faith, or else to incur the reproach of having deserted from their subscriptions, the suspicion of insincerity," and so forth.[1]

[1] For an account of the petition, and of the debate on Sir W.

It is not uninstructive to notice how the arguments which may now be heard in the House of Commons on a Wednesday afternoon were anticipated a hundred years since. First, there were the people who, like Sir Roger Newdigate, " ridiculed the alleged scruples of conscience of the clergy, and said that it was such tender consciences that in the last century subverted the Church." Then came the trimmers—the safe men—the subtle people who like to run with the hare and hunt with the hounds—who warmly approve of toleration, only they do not like tolerating. Mr. Hans Stanley may be taken as the type of these persons. He " delivered his sentiments with great moderation," we are told—moderation apparently consisting in the art of admitting the premisses, and then denying the conclusion. The petition appeared to him to involve a contradiction which rendered it an unfit object for the deliberation of the House. This fatal contradiction lay in the fact that " a minority in

Meredith's motion for receiving it, see Adolphus's *George III.* vol. i. pp. 503—508. An attempt was made the following year (1773) by Dr. Porteous and others to review the Liturgy, in such a sense as to counteract the " extravagant projects " of the petitioners of the Feathers Tavern. Particularly the 17th Article was to be rendered more clear and perspicuous, an achievement which has unhappily never yet been effected.

number came to solicit from the majority a material alteration in religion." Here is evidently a most truly outrageous contradiction, which needs no comment. "Professing himself a warm friend to toleration, he resisted the right of separate sectaries to teach ecclesiastical doctrines under the garb of the Church of England." Want of time or some other reason prevented him from stating in detail the exact texture, and colour, and fashion of this garb. He wound up with convenient vagueness by pronouncing it "inconsistent and dangerous to introduce such a proposition to Parliament; for, although a free country may alter any law, being the creature of the Legislature, yet there are laws so fundamental that they cannot be altered without shaking the basis of the State." These arguments, we should remember, are directed not against the claim of the clergy only, but against releasing civil lawyers, doctors, and other learned men. And this is the side on which Burke fought, zealous then as he was seventeen years later against encouraging freedom of thought, and ever leaning towards prescription, custom, grooves, and the Church, "exalting her mitred front in Court and Parliament."

Burke, of course, was much too well read in the history of the English Church to echo Mr. Hans

Stanley's nonsense about the difference between laws that are the creatures of the Legislature, and those which, like the Acts of Uniformity, are too fundamental to be altered. He expressly admitted that " the Church, like every body corporate, may alter her laws without changing her identity." [1] This argument was strong enough, as against the case of the clerical petitioners, for they expressly declared their willingness to accept a compulsory subscription to the

---

[1] It seems worth while, in the face of the laughable pretensions now being made by a certain party in the Church, to quote the whole of this passage. "Two honourable gentlemen assert that if you alter her symbols you destroy the being of the Church of England. This, for the sake of the liberty of that Church, I most absolutely deny. As an independent Church, professing fallibility, she has claimed the right of acting without the consent of any other ; as a Church, she claims, and has always exercised, a right of reforming whatever appeared amiss in her doctrine, her discipline, or her rites. She did so when she shook off the Papal supremacy in the reign of Henry VIII. which was an act of the body of the Church as well as the State (I don't inquire how obtained). She did so when she twice changed her liturgy in the reign of King Edward ; when she then established articles which were themselves a variation from former professions. She did so when she cut off three articles from her original forty-two, and reduced them to the present thirty-nine ; and she certainly would not lose her corporate identity, nor subvert her fundamental principles, though she were to leave ten of the thirty-nine which remain out of any future confession of her faith. She would limit her corporate powers, on the contrary, and she would oppose her fundamental principles, if she were to deny herself the prudential exercise of such capacity of reformation."— *Speech on the Acts of Uniformity*, Works, ii. 465, 466.

Scriptures.   Burke instantly saw the weakness of this.
" What is the Scripture," he asked, triumphantly, " to
which they are content to subscribe ? "   All depends
on a man's canon; and who can limit the diversity
of the canons ?   To ascertain what Scripture is, you
must have another article; and when you have made
up your mind what it is, you must then ascertain
also what conclusions a man draws from it before
you send him down with the authority of the State
to teach them as pure doctrine, and to receive a tenth
of the produce of our lands in return.   " For," he
continues, with unanswerable cogency, " the Scripture
is no one summary of doctrines regularly digested,
in which a man could not mistake his way : it is a
most venerable, but most multifarious collection of
the records of the Divine economy——a collection of
an infinite variety of cosmogony, theology, history,
prophecy, psalmody, morality, apologue, allegory, legislature, ethics — carried through different books, by
different authors at different ages, for different ends
and purposes."

Neither the conception of a National Church, nor
the conviction of the inexpediency of any Subscription at all, had then ripened as they have done since.
The former, at least, was then unknown, and the latter

was not understood in the sense which we understand it now. It is worth noticing how this controversy, like so many others, has thus moved from the grounds on which it was conducted in the last century. Burke himself accepted Locke's definition of the Church as a voluntary society, and argued justly on this definition that it is essential to exclude from such a voluntary society any member whom she thinks fit to exclude, or to resist the entrance of any upon such conditions as she thinks proper. Otherwise, " it would be a voluntary society acting contrary to her will, which is a contradiction in terms." By this time, however, we have found out that to call it a voluntary society, is not to give an entirely adequate account of a corporation to which we are compelled to contribute, or else have our goods distrained upon if we decline.

Perhaps this may seem already too long a digression, although it is always the most instructive of all processes for our own guidance to discover the different attitudes which are assumed in different generations towards the same question. There is one passage, however, in Burke's speech on the Acts of Uniformity, for the sake of which I digressed in the first instance, and which I must not omit. The spirit of religious controversy, he was arguing, has slackened by the nature of things; by a deliberate act, such as relaxing Subscription, you will revive it. And then he says, " I will not enter into the question how much truth is preferable to peace. Perhaps truth may be far better. But as we have scarcely ever the same certainty in the one that we have in the other, I would, unless the truth were evident indeed, hold fast to peace, which has in his company charity, the highest of the virtues." [1] His appreciation of the highest virtue was shown in the following year, as we have already seen, by his menaces against those just objects of vengeance, those wicked victims of the shafts of the law and the terrors of government. Apart from this, there is nothing more characteristic in all Burke's writings of his steadfast adherence to the principle of *quieta non movere* throughout his career, than this deliberate preference of peace over truth, unless the truth be evident indeed. As if every truth that is worth having had not been the source of strife and contest—as if every truth-seeker did not come, not to bring peace but a sword—and as if every belief to which at any given time we cling most firmly had not passed through

[1] Works, ii. 468, *a.*

a stage when it was far from being evident indeed. Burke was right in his conviction that we hold our beliefs for their own sake, for the comfort and enjoyment they contain, and not for the sake of constantly examining them and proving them. But his natural bent united with the circumstances in which he was placed to make him blind to the fact that what makes one generation better than another is the fruit of examination, and of the greater and deeper knowledge which results from examination. I do not know of any passage in Burke's writings which shows a philosophic estimation of the value of absolutely unfettered inquiry. He could say, indeed, that " our antagonist is our helper," but only within certain bounds. Beyond these the antagonist was a just object of vengeance.

There is no part of Burke's career at which we may not find evidence of his instinctive and undying repugnance to the critical or revolutionary spirit and all its works. From the early days when he had parodied Bolingbroke, down to the later time when he denounced Condorcet as a " fanatic atheist," with " every disposition to the lowest as well as the highest and most determined villanies,"[1] he consistently detested and

[1] *Thoughts on French Affairs*, Works, i. 574, *b*, and 579, *b*.

despised everybody, virtuous or vicious, high-minded or ignoble, who inquired with too keen a scrutiny into the foundations of morals, of religion, of social order. He never swerved in his antipathy to free thought, whether in politics, in theology, or in ethics. To examine with a curious or unfavourable eye the bases of established opinions was to show a leaning to anarchy in one order, to atheism in another, to unbridled libertinism in the third.

In every man there is a certain inevitable connexion of opinion. We hold our views by sets and series. If we espouse one, we have unconsciously let in along with this a little, or it may be a long, train of others. A man comes to a certain conclusion upon some greatly controverted point of science. His eye has possibly never turned aside from the straitened bounds of scientific matter, and yet his single conclusion here leads him insensibly to a whole parcel of conclusions in religious matter or in ethical matter. We ought to remember this in the case of Burke. Few men's opinions hang together so closely and compactly as his did. The fiery glow of his nature fused all his ideas into a tenacious and homogeneous mass. What in more commonplace minds is effected by a process of bad logic, or by what seems to be hazard and caprice, in him was wrought by an inborn ardour of character. His passionate enthusiasm for Order—and this is not a jot more strong in the *Reflections*, in 1790, than it was in the *Thoughts on the Present Discontents* twenty years before—subjugated him as profoundly in one field as in another, in theology as in philosophy, in speculation as in practical politics. In that restlessness to which the world is so deeply indebted in some respects, by which it has been so much injured in others, Burke could recognise but scanty merit, wherever it was exhibited. Himself the most industrious, the most active-minded of men, he was ever sober in fixing the limits, in cutting the channels of his activity, and he would fain have had others equally moderate. Abstract illimitable speculation had no attraction for him in any of its departments. Perceiving that plain and righteous conduct is the end of life in this world, he prayed men not to be over-curious in searching for, and handling, and again handling, the theoretic base on which the prerogatives of virtue repose. Perceiving that the happiness of a people is the end of its government, he abhorred equally the royal clique who took the end of government to be the gratification of the royal will, the old Whig clique who took it to be the enrichment of old Whigs, and the

revolutionists, who, as Burke thought, supposed that
the happiness of a people could never be secure save
where there is no government, but only anarchy.   Perceiving that the belief in a future life with changed
conditions adds dignity to mortals in their hours of
happiness, and brings comfort in their hours of anguish,
and that the belief in a divine mediator may be in the
same way a source of elevation and solace, he burned
with a holy rage against men who seemed to him
as thieves wantonly robbing humanity of its most
precious treasures.   Provided that there was peace,
that is to say, general happiness and content,
Burke felt that a too great inquisitiveness as to its
foundations was not only idle, but mischievous and
cruel.

We have already seen how he considered the
comparative strength of the claims upon us of truth
and peace to be an open question.   "As we have
scarcely ever the same certainty in the one as we
have in the other, I would, unless the truth were
evident indeed, hold fast to peace."   In another place,
he exclaims in precisely the same spirit, "The bulk of
mankind, on their part, are not exceedingly curious
concerning any theories, whilst they are really happy ;
and one sure symptom of an ill-conducted state is the

propensity of the people to resort to them."[1]   And
Burke thought the bulk of mankind in the right.
Even in a state of things which the most eager of
optimists would have hesitated to look on as a state of
peace, Burke was always careful to approach the ailing
organ, whether ecclesiastical or political, with that
awe and reverence, as he expressed it, with which a
young physician approaches to the cure of the disorders
of his aged parent.[2]   Every institution or idea under
which any mass of men found shelter or comfort, he
regarded with this filial awe and affectionate reverence.
I feel an insuperable reluctance, he said in one place,
in giving my hand to destroy any established institution of Government upon a theory, however plausible
it may be.[3]   Rightly conceiving that a stable equilibrium in society, or peace, as he always called it, is the
aim and standard of all things, he was willing to believe
in some mysterious finality of Nature, whom he supposed to have established once for all in 1688 the
entire conditions of our national health.   He habitually
confounded existing usage and traditions, to be gently
modified and tenderly repaired, if unfortunate occasion

[1] *Letter to the Sheriffs of Bristol,* Works, i. 218, *a.*
[2] *Speech on Economical Reform,* Works, i. 238, *a.*
[3] Works, i. 276, *a.*

should require, with a moral and just equilibrium. The philosophic partisan of Order, who entreats men to be sure they get the best out of the systems under which the time constrains them to live, before casting recklessly about for new things, commonly receives something less than justice from the anxious and ardent partisans of Progress. And this has perhaps been Burke's lot. Men constitutionally, or by habit, unable to realise the pleasures conferred by a reverent love of political, social, and moral order, have dealt little sympathy to one who threw himself so consistently and vehemently as Burke did athwart the revolutionary or critical movement of his time. But those of us, who are not estopped by vain shibboleths from protesting that living, after all, must be the end of life, and that stable peace must be the end of society, may see that Burke's horror of the critical spirit in all its various manifestations, was the intelligible pain of one in the ghastly presence of dissolution, not knowing that the angel of a new life is already at his side.

Bishop Watson was probably only one of many who observed very early that this was the unmistakeable temper of Burke's mind. " I admired, as everybody did," he says, " the talents, but not the principles of Mr. Burke ; his opposition to the Clerical Petition first excited my suspicion of his being a High Churchman in religion, and a Tory, perhaps an aristocratic Tory, in the State." [1] Watson, under the singularly grotesque name of a Christian Whig, had written in defence of the petition against Subscription (1772), and may therefore be supposed to have been more acute than his neighbours in detecting the latent tendencies of a conspicuous opponent. It may also be worth noticing, that the person who thus early found out the consistency and coherence of Burke's political system, was destined himself to become a remarkable type of that very inconsistency of which Burke is so constantly and so wrongly accused. After having been all his life one of the most violent and intemperate enemies of things established, alike in Church and State, and even having so late as 1791 delivered a charge to the clergy of his diocese, denouncing the Corporation and Test Acts, and eulogising the French Revolution, Watson suddenly turned right round, and in 1793 published a hateful sermon under the hateful title of *The Wisdom and Goodness of God in having made both Rich and Poor*, in which he denounced

[1] Prior's *Life of Burke*, i. 388.

democratic principles, and bewailed the turn of events
that had obliged him to change his mind.

Nobody can truly understand Burke's character, or
his place among statesmen, without seeing that his
apparent alienation from popular principles was not
in any way due to that turn of events which proved
so fatal to such persons as Watson. He was always
a lover of order in his most enlarged and liberal
moods. He was never more than a lover of order
when his deference to the wishes of the people was
at its lowest. The institutions to which he was
attached during the eight-and-twenty years of his life
in the House of Commons, passed through two phases
of peril. First, they were oppressed and undermined
by the acts of the court, and the resurrection of prerogative in the guise of privilege. Then they were
menaced by the democratic flood which overtook England after the furious rising of the popular tide in
France. We at this distance of time may see that in
neither case was the danger so serious and so real
as it appeared in the eyes of contemporaries. But in
both cases Burke was filled with an alarm that may
serve as a measure of the depth and sincerity of
his reverence for the fabric whose overthrow, as he
thought, was gravely threatened. In both cases he

set his face resolutely against innovation; in both cases he defied the enemies who came up from two different quarters to assail the English constitution, and to destroy a system under which three generations of Englishmen had been happy and prosperous. /He changed his front, but he never changed his ground./ " I flatter myself," he said, with justice, "that I love a manly, moral, regulated liberty."[1] And again: "The liberty, the only liberty I mean, is a liberty connected with order."[2] The court tried to regulate liberty too severely. It found in him an inflexible opponent. Demagogues tried to remove the regulations of liberty. They encountered in him the bitterest and most unceasing of all remonstrants. The arbitrary majority in the House of Commons forgot for whose benefit they held power, from whom they derived their authority, and in what description of government it was that they had a place. Burke was the most valiant and strenuous champion in the ranks of the independent minority. He withstood to the face the King and the King's friends. He withstood to the face Charles Fox and the friends of the people. He may have been wrong in both, or in either, but let

[1] *Reflections,* Works, i. 384, *a.*
[2] *Speech on Arrival at Bristol* (1774), Works, i. 177, *b.*

us not be told that he turned back in his course;
that he was a revolutionist in 1770 and a reactionist
in 1790; that he was in his sane mind when he
opposed the supremacy of the Court, but that his
reason was tottering before he opposed the supremacy
of the rabble.[1]

[1] " As any one of the great members of this constitution happens to
be endangered, he that is a friend to all of them chooses and presses
the topics necessary for the support of the part attacked. . . . He
ought not to apprehend that his raising fences about popular privileges this day will infer that he ought on the next to concur with
those who would pull down the throne; because on the next he
defends the throne, it ought not to be supposed that he has abandoned
the rights of the people." *Appeal from the New to the Old Whigs,*
Works, i. 501, *b.*

CHAPTER II.

ISSUES OF THE TIME.

IS not the highest object of our search in a study of the career of a conspicuous man, an estimate of his contributions to the cause of the collective progress of mankind? We have to ask first, what general advance was made by this cause, while he was still a witness of it; and next, what place and part he took as an actor in it. We seek to know how the ideas and policy of his country affected the progress of history, and we seek to know in what attitude he stood to this policy, and in what respects he modified these ideas. Apart from all this, we may allow, the merely pictorial study of such a man as Burke is profoundly interesting and attractive. We hear him in conversation at the club, with Johnson and Goldsmith, and Reynolds and Windham, winding into his subject like a serpent, as Goldsmith said of him; bidding some too grave and anxious gentleman to "live pleasant;" fascinating the great-hearted Johnson with "his knowledge, his genius, his diffusion and affluence of conversation," and making him cry, "Sir, that fellow calls forth all my powers." We see him in the House of Commons, in his tight brown coat, with his spectacles and a little bob-wig with curls, beginning his oration with folded arms and an air of humility, and gradually rising to thunderous denunciations of the noble lord in the blue ribbon; or later on, of those vain petulant upstarts in a neighbouring country, who were wickedly proscribing the sacred ministers of religion, persecuting their virtuous and innocent sovereign, and covering with humiliation the august daughter of the Cæsars. We may follow him from the heat and violence of the House, where drunken lordlings and squires derided the greatest man of their time, down to the calm shades of Beaconsfield, where he would with his own hands give food to a starving beggar, or medicine to a peasant sick of the ague; where he would talk of the weather, the turnips, and the hay, with the team-men and the farm-bailiff; and where, in the evening stillness, he would pace the walk under the trees, and reflect on the state of Europe and the distractions of his country. While Fox was squandering tens of thousands at the gambling-table, we may watch Burke supporting Barry for several years at Rome; anxiously pressing his last half-guinea upon the friendless Emin ; rescuing Crabbe, though a perfect stranger to him, from a debtors' prison, and maintaining him in his own house until a provision was found for him; and on every occasion ready to extend not only sympathy, but a share of his slender purse, wherever he found penniless genius or worth. And finally, we may look with tragic emotion on the pathos of that crowning. scene which left the remnant of the old man's days so desolate and void. A Roman poet has described, in touching words, the woe of the aged Nestor, as he beheld the funeral-pile of his son, too untimely slain.

" Oro parumper
Attendas quantum de legibus ipse queratur
Fatorum et nimio de stamine, quum videt acris
Antilochi barbam ardentem : quum quærit ab omni
Quisquis adest socius, cur hæc in tempora duret,
Quod facinus dignum tam longo admiserit ævo.''

Burke's grief finds a yet nobler expression. "The storm has gone over me; and I lie like one of those old oaks which the late hurricane has scattered about me. I am stripped of all my honours; I am torn up by the roots, and lie prostrate on the earth. . . . .

I am alone. I have none to meet my enemies in the gate. . . . . I live in an inverted order. They who ought to have succeeded me have gone before me. They who should have been to me as posterity are in the place of ancestors." [1]

And if the votary of pictorial history thus finds an interesting and affecting subject in Burke's life, neither will he be disappointed who studies remarkable men from the moralist's point of view. Burke was irritable and violent, it is true, but even here he sinned out of zeal for the State, and enthusiasm for his principles. They were not private grievances, but public follies and public injuries, which moved him to these impatient outbreaks. There had not been half-a-dozen prominent politicians since the Great Rebellion and the Commonwealth with whom personal objects counted for so absolutely little as they did with Edmund Burke. He really did what so large a majority of public men only feign to do. He forgot that he had any interests of his own to be promoted, apart from the interests of the party with which he acted and from those of the whole nation, for which he held himself a trustee. What William Burke said of him in 1766, was true throughout his life—

[1] *Letter to a Noble Lord*, Works, ii. 268, *a*.

"Ned is full of real business, intent upon doing solid good to his country, as much as if he was to receive twenty per cent. from the commerce of the whole empire, which he labours to extend and improve."[1]

Above all things, he achieved honourable and independent political distinction, at a time when it was much harder for a plebeian to achieve distinction on such terms than it is now. When we remember all the untold bitternesses of the struggle in which he was engaged from the time when the old Duke of Newcastle tried to make the Marquis of Rockingham dismiss his new private secretary as an Irish Jesuit in disguise (1765), down to the time when the Duke of Bedford, himself battening " in grants to the house of Russell, so enormous as not only to outrage economy, but even to stagger credibility," reviled the Government for giving Burke a moderate pension, we may almost imagine that if Johnson had imitated the famous Tenth Satire a little later he would have been tempted to apply the poet's cynical criticism of the career heroic to the greater Cicero of his own day. " I was not," Burke said, in a passage of lofty dignity, " like his Grace of Bedford, swaddled and rocked and dandled into a legislator ; *Nitor in adversum* is the

[1] Prior's *Life of Burke*, i. 151.

motto for a man like me. I possessed not one of the
qualities nor cultivated one of the arts that recommend
men to the favour and protection of the great. I was
not made for a minion or a tool. As little did I follow
the trade of winning the hearts, by imposing on the
understandings of the people. At every step of my
progress in life, for in every step was I traversed and
opposed, and at every turnpike I met, I was obliged
to show my passport, and again and again to prove
my sole title to the honour of being useful to my
country, by a proof that I was not wholly unac-
quainted with its laws and the whole system of its
interests both abroad and at home ; otherwise no rank,
no toleration even for me."[1]

And let us remember the kind of men with whom
he had to compete on these unequal terms. Their
unscrupulous and utterly dishonourable selfishness is
admirably illustrated in one of Walpole's stories.
"The Duke of Grafton," he tells us, "gave a dinner
to several of the principal men in the city to settle
the loan. Mr. Townshend came in his nightgown,
and after dinner, when the terms were settled, and
every one present wished to introduce some friend in
the list of subscribers, he pretended to cast up the

_____

[1] *Letter to a Noble Lord*, Works, ii. 263—4.

sums already subscribed, said the loan was full, huddled up his papers, got into a chaise and returned home, reserving to himself by this manœuvre a large share in the loan."[1] These loans of course were raised on terms as unfavourable to the State as possible, and the gains went into the hands of those who were lucky enough to get the scrip. Romilly mentions a loan made by Lord North, on terms so favourable to the subscribers, and so disadvantageous to the public, therefore, as to have borne the next day a premium of ten per cent., and to have remained afterwards at from ten to seven per cent. premium.[2] Dissoluteness was no drawback in one of the favoured order, any more than corruption and dishonesty. When Fox defended the practice of subscription against clerical and lay recalcitrants, he had prepared himself for that holy war, as Gibbon tells us, " by passing twenty-two hours in the pious exercise of hazard, his devotion only costing him five hundred pounds per hour."[3] When Burke,

[1] Quoted in May's *Constitutional Hist.* i. 324–5.

[2] Romilly's *Life*, i. 120. William Pitt was the first minister who consulted the public interest by accepting the lowest terms that were tendered, without retaining a farthing in his own hands for distribution among his friends (1784). Cf. Stanhope's *Life of Pitt*, i. 220, where Pitt's bold integrity is contrasted with the well-meaning feebleness of Lord Rockingham.

[3] Gibbon's *Miscel. Works*, ii. 74.

exhausted with a day's assiduous labour, used to call
for Fox at his apartments in St. James's, on his way
to the House, he would find him just out of bed,
all bright and fresh for the evening's work.   Such men
as the shrewd and impudent Rigby, on the other hand,
atoned for a plebeian origin by the arts of dependence
and a judicious servility, and drew more of the public
money from the pay office in half-a-dozen quarter-days,
than Burke received in all his life.   It was not by such
arts that Burke rose.   His boast was justifiable.   He
was not made for a minion or a tool of corrupt or
dissolute patricians.   He was still less made for a
flatterer and cajoler of the populace.[1]

Whether, therefore, we are of those who see no more
in the world's great men than conspicuous figures in a
lively and many-coloured scene, or of those others who
love great men for the qualities which, in kind, they
have in common with all their human brothers, and
which spring from the common conditions of human
life, in either case Burke attracts us with equal and
irresistible force.   But history proper is only concerned
with these aspects of the character of its prominent
actors incidentally and by the way.   At the most, they
are only accessories to true historic study, which the

[1] See Note at the end of the Chapter.

painter of manners or the humourist may lend, but which it is a fundamental mistake in thought to confound with the historic study itself. History has strictly only to do with individual men as the originals, the furtherers, the opponents, or the representatives of some of those thousand diverse forces which, uniting in one vast sweep, bear along the successive generations of men as upon the broad wings of sea-winds to new and more fertile shores. No modern epoch has witnessed the beginnings of so many of these important movements as that which is covered by Burke's parliamentary life. In every order of activity a fresh and gigantic impulse was given, the tide of national life widened and swelled under the influence of new and flushed tributaries, the springs and sources were unsealed of modern ideas, modern systems, and of ideas and systems that are still to be developed.

In the Spiritual order, for instance, when Burke was achieving his first successes in the House of Commons (1766), Wesley and Whitefield were strenuously traversing the length and breadth of the land, quickening the deep-hidden sensibilities, and filling with lofty and divine visions the once blind souls of men and women who had laboured blankly, as brute beasts labour, down in coal mines, in factories, over furnaces and forges, in dank fields, on barren, remote moors, and who till then had known no glimpses of a wider and more joyful life than the life of a starved and ever-benumbed sense.

In the Industrial order a development of no less momentous importance dates from the same time. In the year in which Burke published his *Thoughts on the Present Discontents* (1770), Hargreaves took out his patent for the spinning-jenny, the year before that is the date of Arkwright's patent, and nine years later Samuel Crompton invented that wonderful machine, the mule, which endures as a marvel of ingenuity even in our own ingenious times. The improvement of means of transport proceeded at an equal pace with improvements in means of production. For while Burke was pondering his maiden speech (1766), Brindley was beginning the Grand Trunk Canal from the Trent to the Mersey, and Watt was busy on the third model of the steam-engine.

In the Speculative and Scientific order, while Burke and the Rockingham party were marking their abhorrence and despair at the American policy of Lord North and the Court by a partial secession from Parliament (1776), the *Wealth of Nations* was given to the world, and the foundations laid of economic science. Nor should we overlook the important fact that the tremendously powerful solvents supplied by Hume forty years before, were at this time as potent for destruction in one set of opinions as Adam Smith's book was for construction in another set. Thus Burke's contemporaries saw the Wesleyan revival of Christian belief. They saw the rise of a philosophy which directly and indirectly has done more to weaken and narrow that belief than Wesley or Butler, or anybody else did, to restore it. They saw those triumphs of mechanical invention and engineering science which were destined to revolutionise modern life. And, above all, they saw established those theoretic principles of commerce which, overthrowing the old notions of the mercantile system, were to add a thousandfold to the material comfort of mankind, and to prove an indispensable, though rough and temporary means, of propagating the idea of the brotherhood of nations.

Fourthly, and finally, in the Political order. The year which saw the *Wealth of Nations* (1776), saw also the Declaration of American Independence. The year before Burke wrote the Letter to the Sheriffs of Bristol, Franklin was consoling Jefferson by the story of John Thompson the hatter, for the changes

F

made by their colleagues in Jefferson's draft of the Declaration,[1] and shortly afterwards they all agreed upon that ever memorable announcement, " We, therefore, the representatives of the United States of America, in general congress assembled, appealing to the Supreme Judge of the world for the rectitude of our intentions, do in the name and by the authority of the good people of these colonies, solemnly publish and declare that these united colonies are, and of right ought to be, Free and Independent States." Thirteen years later, "the evening sun of July" shone over the blood-stained ruin of the Bastille. The foundation of the new republic and the uprooting of the old monarchy were the two great events in the political order. Each is an achievement that in its relation to ourselves and some generations of our descendants, can have no rival in importance save the other.

Though for the purposes of analysis and clear classification it is essential that we should speak of each of these impulses as single and distinct, it is highly important that we should recognise their common direction. Each of them is one element in the history of the country, but all the elements receive a common

[1] **Earl** Stanhope's *History of England.* vol. vi. p. 97. (Fifth Edition.)

suffusion, which we are content vaguely to call the spirit of the times. Every age has its strong setting current of ideas. Those movements only retain a permanent interest which are in harmony with this current. Isolated fragments of antipathetic effort, spasmodic outbreaks of counter endeavour, pass away and are lost. It is the composition and fusion of main forces which arrest the eye of the historian.

It is not necessary for me to show in detail how the spirit of the Wesleyan reformation fitted in with the characteristic movements of the time. It is enough to commemorate the aid given to industrial development by the increase of thrift, sobriety, diligence, and those other moral virtues, a disposition to which was borne into the heart along with the newly-awakened spirit of religious fervour. The development of democratic principles was just as powerfully, though less palpably and visibly, helped forward by the Christian revival in the eighteenth century, as it has been by every system which calls the individual to think, and makes him responsible, at the peril of his soul, for the results of his thinking. In England, moreover, dissent from the Established Church has always been more or less democratic, because the Church is the emblem and ally of authority. The way in which the discoveries of

Adam Smith fitted in with the great mechanical inventions that were made at the same time is too obvious to need dwelling upon. To perceive clearly, first, that manufactures enrich, not impoverish a country, and second, that manufactures thrive better where there are the fewest restrictions on the free interchange of commodities—first, to assert the power of manufactures in increasing the national wealth, and second, to establish the conditions under which this power can rise to the greatest height of efficiency—this was the natural accompaniment in theory to the inventions of Arkwright and Crompton and Watt in practice. Still less need I devote any words to establish the underlying connexion which subsists between a vigorous industrial movement and the impulse towards the abolition of privilege. Any ordinary House of Commons politician knows that the artisans are, as a class, the resolute enemies of Privilege, though perhaps barely resolute enough. The vigorous growth of manufactures is indirectly as fatal to favoured orders, as the foundation of the American Republic and the French Revolution were directly.

These, then, were the two prime characteristics which sum up the tendencies of Burke's age : an enormous development of industry, and the first germs of a substitution of the government of a whole people by itself for the exploded and tottering system of government by privileged orders. The seeds thus sown have come up with unequal rapidity, yet their maturity will not improbably be contemporaneous. The organisation of Labour and the overthrow of Privilege are tasks which we may expect to see perfected at the same time, because most of the conditions that lie about the root of the one are also at the foundation of the other. When we can grapple with the moral confusion that reigns in one field, the obstacles in the other will no longer discourage or baffle us.

A statesman may well be pardoned for not discerning the germs of new things about his feet : he too often fails to see them even when they have grown breast high. It is but little reproach to him not to have descried the small cloud on the remote horizon no bigger than a man's hand, when he so often moves in serene unconsciousness of the tempest ready to burst over his head. But the truly wise man, to whom posterity may avow a debt of gratitude, even if he be not keen-sighted enough to see the direction in which the distant lines of the future are stretching, will always be enough in harmony with the best influences of his time to spend his activity in unconscious pre-

paration for the new state. This was the case with
Burke. He did not see whither the moral and political
agencies of his day were ultimately tending. He did
not understand that there were conditions in active
operation which would, in the long run, entirely dis-
solve into air his conception of the best government
as an aristocracy of birth with popular sympathies.
But he was sufficiently alive to the force of these conditions, and sufficiently sensible of the virtue that was
in them, to expend his energies in a way that did much
to prepare an easier opening for the consummation of
an end which, in the form that it then threatened to
assume, he openly abhorred. Sansculottism in Burke's
day, as in our own, was habitually identified with
democracy. A democrat in society and elsewhere was
always taken for a Jacobin. This spurious imitation
of a free national government naturally excited the
utmost repugnance in the mind of such a partisan of
order as Burke was. But, however unconsciously, he
did his best to prepare the way for the advent of the
true Democracy, by insisting, at a time when the
popular sympathies of the privileged classes were luke-
warm or extinct, that government existed for the
people, and that the will of the people is the irresistible
master of those to whom it has entrusted the guardian-

ship of its rights. He had one supreme idea. This was the adaptation of the established order of government to the wants and the interests of the governed. There were thus two objects of his reverence, the established order of things, and the wishes and welfare of those for whom the established order existed. Until the French Revolution, the circumstances of his country made the popular interest most prominent in his mind. Then the Revolution came, and all his solicitude was for the established order of things. The time has perhaps not yet come for us to characterise this tremendous convulsion. It would be useless to attempt to strike a balance between the service which Burke rendered to the cause of Progress by his consistent advocacy of popular principles until 1790, and the ill which he did afterwards by helping to organise the terrors of the panic-stricken rulers of the country into an instrument for a long reign of political repression and absolutism. Let us, first, at all events, confine our attention to the part that Burke played in the constitutional struggles which began with the accession of George III. and which raged, at last in the shape of Regency Debates, up to the very year of the great outbreak that extinguished them for nearly forty years to come.

Until the accession of Pitt in 1783, there were three leading issues. The first concerned the relations between the sovereign and the chambers; the second, between the chambers and the people ; and the third, between the sovereign and the chambers, and the executive. The question in the first case was, whether the will of the sovereign or the vote of the chamber should be the final and decisive appeal in great affairs of State ; whether the sovereign, under the thin and temporary disguise of Influence, should be the true dictator and autocrat over the legislature, while the latter dwindled into the submissive registrar of his decrees ; or whether the House of Commons should become the supreme organ, the chief centre of force and energy, the seat of the most vital functions, in the governing system. The second issue was, whether the House of Commons should assume that arbitrary and indisputable authority over the people which the King aspired to assume over the House, or whether the desires and opinions of the whole people should be the ultimate guide and standard of legislative action. The third issue was, whether the ministry of the day should be a solidly compacted body, acting on some one common principle of policy, all standing together, all falling together, and corporately responsible to the House of

Commons, or whether each minister should be content with the direction of the affairs of his own department, deriving the spirit of his instructions not from the House but from the King, and being to the King only responsible.

There were thus three points, as it were, at which the same contest of principles was being carried on,—three aspects of the old and only half-settled conflict between the popular and the arbitrary theories of the Constitution. In short, a revolution was being accomplished. It is now plain that nothing less than revolutionary issues were involved — the supremacy of the House of Commons in the legislature and over the executive, and the supremacy of the popular wishes in the House of Commons. This must constantly be borne in mind by all who wish to see the bottom of the events of the period. Viewed in the merely personal light these events are unintelligible, and it is not until we thus discern the principles at stake, that the history of the time assumes a meaning. The whole history of this reign, perhaps from its nearness to us, has been so overloaded with a mass of trumpery personal anecdotes, and attention has been so exclusively paid to the constant shufflings and combinations going on among Grenvilles and Bedfords,

Rockinghams and Shelburnes, that people have over-looked the true importance of the crisis, and have too often failed to distinguish the vital from the accidental features of the first twenty years after the accession of George III.　This crisis was only the preliminary stage of the greater revolution which is going silently forward in our own days.　But it was an indispensable stage, and a man was or was not amenable to the best influences of the time, was or was not in accord with its best conditions, according to the side he took in this contest.

Burke from the first seized the true significance of the position.　He strenuously supported the free side of the Constitution, and aroused and reinvigorated its champions.　In every part of the field he was the noblest vindicator of the supremacy of the will of the whole people.　" To follow, not to force, the public inclination ; to give a direction, a form, a technical dress, and a specific sanction to the general sense of the community," he declared to be the true end of legislature.[1]　" The virtue, spirit, and essence of a House of Commons consists," he said, " in its being the express image of the feelings of the nation." [2]　And in

[1] *Letter to the Sheriffs of Bristol*, Works, i. 216, *a.*
[2] *Thoughts on Present Discontents*, Works, i. 114, *b.*

the same spirit he insisted that "the House of Commons can never be a control on other parts of government, unless they are controlled themselves by their constituents." [1]

NOTE, p. 62.

In a bad book, Schlosser's *History of the Eighteenth Century,* Burke is called Rockingham's creature, an Irish adventurer, and so forth, and it is said that "the aristocratic families, in order to be sure of him, provided at their cost, economically, for his housekeeping." The author's accurate familiarity with Burke's life and history may be seen in one or two instances which I have noted down. Whenever he exchanges rhapsodical invective for plain statement he makes a blunder. 1. *His work upon the Sublime and Beautiful, which appeared in 1757.* It was in 1756. 2. *Burke was accordingly returned for one of Lord Rockingham's boroughs in 1765.* He was returned for *Lord Verney's* borough of Wendover, and Lord Rockingham had nothing to do with it. 3. *Towards the end of the time fixed for this parliament* [*i.e.* the parliament sitting in 1765], *he came out with a speech on the occasion of the Boston Port Bill.* Considering that the Boston Por Bill was brought forward in 1774, and that this parliament was dissolved in March, 1768, how does he make this out? 4. *As an orator Burke appeared for the first time on an occasion very favourable to his reputation; this was in March and April,* 1774. The accurate German is here eight years wrong. Burke's first speech was January 27, 1766. It created a great impression, and Pitt congratulated Burke's party on his accession. 5. *In a speech delivered on the 19th April,* 1774, *in support of Rose Fuller's motion Burke expressed himself against this small tax. . . . Burke already appears very different in his second elaborate and renowned speech on North American affairs, delivered on the 15th November,* 1775. Burke made

[1] *Thoughts on Present Discontents,* Works, i. 143, *b.*

no speech at all on the 15th of November, and though he did make one on the 16th, nobody in this world ever did or could pretend that it was elaborate or renowned either. The speech Schlosser means is no doubt that of the 22nd of March, on Conciliation with America—perhaps the noblest, wisest, and weightiest of all Burke's pieces.

Some sordid imputations have been in recent times thrown upon Burke's honour and credit, with reference, first to the Clogher Estate, and second to the purchase of Beaconsfield. If anybody cares to see them thoroughly and finally overthrown in a clear and legal manner, with references to conclusive documents, I may refer him to the Right Hon. J. Napier's lecture on Burke, delivered before the Dublin Young Men's Christian Association, in 1862, p. 51 *et seq.*

CHAPTER III.

THE CONSTITUTION.

IT has been incidentally observed by Mr. Hallam that the Revolution was the means of establishing a semi-republican scheme of constitutional law in the English Parliament.[1] Judicious as this remark is, still it does not carry us the whole way towards the important truth about the change in feeling which the Revolution had thus occasioned. The House of Commons, it is true, became animated with a conviction of their own supremacy, that could only be harmonised with a semi-republican scheme. But as it was to the royal supremacy that the Revolution had made them heirs and legatees, so it was in the old royal spirit that they conceived the nature, and set up the expansive boundary-marks, of their own authority. The King's Prerogative was the only pattern they possessed, after which they could model this new fabric of Privilege

---

[1] *Const. Hist.* iii. 406. (Tenth Edition.)

of Parliament.   The conception of authority which shaped itself in their minds was in most of its elements the same as that which in its monarchic expression had been shattered at the Revolution.   Arbitrary ideas were tacitly transplanted from the royal closet to the House of Commons, and the new scheme which sprung from these ideas in their enlarged atmosphere was not perceptibly less anti-popular than the old scheme in which they had been embodied under Plantagenets, Tudors, and Stuarts.   There was nothing about either the actors or the events of the Revolution to favour the growth of republican principles in the sense in which they are now received and in which, owing to circumstances which I will mention in their place, they were received in America. England, after the Revolution, may truly be said to have become a republic, but it was not a republic of the popular type.

The first great constitutional case after Burke came into Parliament was that of John Wilkes and the electors of Middlesex. Parliament, approaching the expiry of its legal term, was dissolved in the spring of 1768. Wilkes, then an outlaw in Paris, returned to England, and announced himself as a candidate for the City. When the election was over his name stood last on the poll. But his ancient fame as the opponent and victim of the Court five years before again awoke, and after his rejection in the City he found himself strong enough to stand for the county of Middlesex. Here, after a very excited election, he was returned at the head of the poll, having 1,292 votes against 827 for Cooke, the next candidate, who thus became his colleague. Dying shortly afterwards, Cooke was replaced by Wilkes's friend, Sergeant Glynn.

The next step in this extraordinary episode in English history was the reversal of his outlawry by Lord Mansfield, followed by the affirmation of the original verdict and the sentence of imprisonment for a couple of years, and the payment of a fine, for the famous Number Forty-five of the *North Briton* in the first place, and the Essay on Woman in the second.

Wilkes was in prison when the second session of the new Parliament began. His case came before the House in November, 1768, on his own petition, accusing Lord Mansfield of altering the record at his trial ; and after many acrimonious debates and examinations of Wilkes and others at the bar of the House, at length, by 219 votes against 136, the famous motion was passed—" That John Wilkes, Esq., a member of this House, who hath at the bar of this House confessed himself to be the author and publisher of what this House has resolved to be an insolent, scandalous, and seditious libel, and who has been convicted in the Court of King's Bench of having printed and published a seditious libel, and three obscene and impious libels, and by the judgment of the said court has been sentenced to undergo twenty-two months' imprisonment, and is now in execution under the same judgment, be *expelled this House.*" The three obscene and impious libels were the Essay on Woman, a parody of the *Veni Creator*, and a commentary on the Essay on Woman, after the manner of Warburton's notes on Pope. The seditious libel was Number Forty-five; while the libel resolved by the House to be insolent, scandalous, and seditious was a comment published by Wilkes, from prison, upon a letter from Lord Weymouth, the Secretary of State, to the Surrey magistrates, recommending them to call in military force to suppress riots in the bud. Wilkes, so far from denying the authorship of this inflammatory document, invited the thanks of his country for denouncing " that bloody scroll." This was the crowning offence, and it led to the resolution to expel him.

The next thing done by the Middlesex freeholders was immediately to re-elect Wilkes without opposition

The day after the return, the House of Commons resolved by an immense majority, " that having been expelled, Mr. Wilkes was incapable of serving in that parliament." The following month Wilkes was once more elected. The House once more declared the election void. In April another election took place, and this time the Government put forward Colonel Luttrell, who vacated his seat for Bossiney for the purpose of opposing Wilkes. There was the same result. For the fourth time Wilkes was at the head of the poll, the votes being 1,143 against 296. The House ordered the return to be altered, and after hearing by counsel the freeholders of Middlesex who petitioned against the alteration, finally confirmed it (May 8, 1760) by a majority of 221 to 152, the greatest majority, according to Lord Temple, ever known the last day of a session.[1]

The purport and significance of these arbitrary proceedings need little interpretation. The House, according to the authorities, had a constitutional right to

---

[1] The *Annual Register* and the *Gentleman's Magazine* contain good contemporary accounts of these transactions. Adolphus, in his first volume, tells the story intelligibly and briefly, and as his observations are in the Tory sense, they are worth looking at, as presenting a slightly different view from that of standard historians of the other side, like Earl Stanhope, who is only half a Tory, and Mr. Massey.

expel Wilkes, though the grounds on which even this
is defended would probably be questioned if a similar
case were to arise in our own day. But a single
branch of the legislature could have no power to
pass an incapacitating vote either against Wilkes or
anybody else. An Act of Parliament is the least instrument by which such incapacity could be imposed.
The House might perhaps expel Wilkes, but it could
not either legally or with regard to the less definite
limits of constitutional morality, decide whom the
Middlesex freeholders should not elect, and it could not
therefore set aside their representative, who was then
free from any disabling quality. Lord Camden did not
much exaggerate when he declared in a debate on the
subject in the House of Lords, that the judgment
passed upon the Middlesex election had given the constitution a more dangerous wound than any which
were given during the twelve years' absence of parliament in the reign of Charles I. The House of
Commons was usurping another form of that very
dispensing power for pretending to which the last
of the Stuart sovereigns had lost his crown. If
the House by a vote could deprive Wilkes of a
right to sit, what legal or constitutional impediment
would there be in the way if the majority were at

any time disposed to declare all their most formidable opponents in the minority incapable of taking their seats?

The King of course was delighted. His letters to Lord North at this time are full of the kind of complacency with which a dull arbitrary man sees the success of his projects. He begins by expressing his opinion " that it is highly proper to apprize you that the expulsion of Mr. Wilkes appears to be very essential, and *must be effected.*" Then, " Nothing could afford me greater pleasure than your account of the great majority last night," when Wilkes's petition was taken into account. On another occasion: " It gives me great pleasure that you have so far got through the fatiguing business." When the alteration in the return was finally voted, the King wrote that " the House of Commons, having in so spirited a manner felt what they owe to their own privileges, as well as to the good order of this country and metropolis, gives me great satisfaction, and must greatly tend to destroy that outrageous licentiousness that has been so successfully raised by wicked and disappointed men ;" and finally assured his minister that " the House of Commons has with becoming dignity supported their own privileges "—George III.'s ignorance and station raised him *super grammaticam*—" without which they could not subsist." Lastly, in the manner of the most inimitable beadle, " It is now my duty with firmness to see the laws obeyed, which I trust will by degrees restore good order, without which no state can flourish."[1]

David Hume, as if to illustrate and justify Burke's uniform contempt for speculative philosophers in practical politics, writing to Dr. Blair, says among other things, that " this madness about Wilkes excited first indignation, then apprehension ; but has gone to such a height, that all other sentiments with me are buried in ridicule. This exceeds the absurdity of Titus Oates and the Popish Plot, and is so much more disgraceful to the nation, as the former folly being derived from religion, flowed from a source which has from uniform prescription acquired a right to impose nonsense on all nations and ages. But the present extravagance is peculiar to ourselves, and quite risible."[2] This is neither the first nor the last time that a learned man has seen nothing but what is quite risible in the instinctive sympathies of the prole-

---

[1] *Correspondence of George III. with Lord North*, i. 2—10. Edited by W. B. Donne.

[2] Burton's *Life of Hume*, ii. 422.

tarians with resistance to an oppressive and lawless oligarchy. Wilkes was but a poor hero, it is true, yet he was a better man than the vile Sandwich,— first his accomplice, and then his betrayer; he was politically as respectable as Lord North, who pandered to the passions of a vulgar monarch quite as recklessly as Wilkes at any time pandered to the passions of a vulgar mob. The violent riots to which the proceedings against Wilkes gave rise, are described by historians in the usual way, as outbreaks of wicked popular rage and extravagance, unaccountable in their origin, and indefensible in their nature and progress. Students are imposed upon by vague talk about the frenzy of the multitude, as if that were an adequate and exhaustive explanation of a rising which at one time was very near being a revolt. The London multitude grew zealous for Wilkes, for the same reason that made the Roman multitude grow zealous for Clodius. Wilkes, it is true, had written filthy verses, and Clodius had been found peeping at the mysteries of the Bona Dea. The crowd, perhaps, cared no more about this than their betters cared about the villanies of Sandwich, or in after days about the carouses and debaucheries of the Prince of Wales. They were themselves sunk in misery, oppressed by cruel and barbarous laws, the victims of every curse that it is in the power of gross misrule to inflict. For this reason they made common cause with one who was accidentally a more conspicuous sufferer. Wilkes was quite right when he vowed that he was no Wilkite. As is often the case, the masses were better than their leader. "Whenever the people have a feeling," Burke once said, "they commonly are in the right : they sometimes mistake the physician." Franklin, who was then in London, was of opinion that if George III. had had a bad character, and John Wilkes a good one, the latter might have turned the former out of the kingdom. Character had less to do with the result than the fact that George III. had the military and material strength of the Government to back him, a strength which he agreed with Lord Weymouth in thinking could never be brought into play soon enough. And after all, if we can only get out of the glare of the Throne, we may agree that on the whole the patricians had about as little to be proud of in George III. as the mob had in Wilkes.

It is impossible to see the meaning of the troubles which sprang from the contest between Wilkes and the oligarchic Lower House more clearly and fully than Burke saw it. Perhaps it would be difficult to characterise it more truly. " I am not one of those," he began, " who think that the people are never wrong. They have been so, frequently and outrageously, both in other countries and in this. But I do say that *in all disputes between them and their rulers, the presumption is at least upon a par in favour of the people.*" Nay, experience perhaps justifies him in going further. When popular discontents are prevalent, something has generally been found amiss in the constitution or the administration. " The people have no interest in disorder. When they go wrong, it is their error, and not their crime." And then he quotes the famous passage from the Memoirs of Sully, which both practical politicians and political students should bind about their necks, and write upon the tables of their hearts, " *Les révolutions qui arrivent dans les grands états ne sont point un effet du hazard, ni du caprice des peuples. . . . Pour la populace, ce n'est jamais par envie d'attaquer qu'elle se soulève, mais par impatience de souffrir.*"[1] This was the secret of Wilkism. It was the protest of the people against the corruption and oppression of its oligarchic

---

[1] *Present Discontents*, Works, i. 125, b.

rulers, and the misery and despair which their iniquitous laws entailed.

It was not only in the splendid pamphlet on the
Present Discontents that Burke showed his keen
appreciation of the true character of the struggle
between Wilkes and the House of Commons.   He put
the case still more plainly in a speech delivered in his
place in 1771.   " The question amounts to this," he told
the House : " whether you mean to be a legal tribunal,
or an arbitrary and despotic assembly."   The issue was
indeed nothing less than this.   It was the second
of those three revolutionary questions which, as I have
said, resume the constitutional history of England from
the accession of George III. to the outbreak of the
French Revolution.   " They are the mortal enemies of
the House of Commons," Burke exclaimed, " who
would persuade them to think or to act as if they were
a self-originated magistracy, independent of the people,
and unconnected with their opinions and feelings."
But these mortal enemies of its very constitution were
at this time the majority of the House.   It was to
no purpose that Burke argued with more than legal
closeness that incapacitation could not be a power
according to law, inasmuch as it had neither of the two
properties of law : it was not *known*, " you yourselves

not knowing upon what grounds you will vote the incapacity of any man;" and it was not *fixed*, because it was varied according to the occasion, exercised according to discretion, and no man could call for it as a right. A strain of unanswerable reasoning of this kind counted for nothing, in spite of its being unanswerable. Despotic or oligarchic pretensions are always proof against the most formidable battery that reason and experience can construct against them.[1] And Wilkes's exclusion endured until this Parliament—the Unreported Parliament, as it was called, and in many respects the very worst that ever assembled at Westminster—was dissolved, and a new one elected (1774), when he was once again returned for Middlesex, and took his seat.

The conduct of one of the sheriffs may serve to illustrate the just and righteous strength of feeling which prevailed on Wilkes's exclusion. Sheriff Townshend was member for the borough of Calne, and in February, 1770, in Committee of Ways and Means, he protested against the House granting the land tax for

[1] Pitt, writing to his mother in 1780, talks of a debate in the House of Commons, "where, according to the old custom, which is, I fear, pretty nearly re-established, arguments and numbers were almost equally clear on opposite sides."—Earl Stanhope's *Life*, i. 40.

the county of Middlesex. The freeholders of that county, he said, by their election, " signed indentures to Mr. Wilkes, giving and granting to him the power of levying taxes upon them. They say Mr. Wilkes, our lawful representative, is kept out of this House by force and violence ; the House itself has set up another candidate in opposition to him, and in so doing has proceeded contrary to the law of the land. Mr. Luttrell is not the representative of the county of Middlesex." The speaker went on to say that he for one would not pay the land tax so levied, and he did his best to keep his word.[1] In November of the same year he was distrained upon for two hundred pounds. He instituted proceedings against the collector, and the trial came off in the King's Bench, before Lord Mansfield. The jury were told that the question was whether there was any legislative power in the county ; if so, then they ought to find for the tax-gatherer. Of course the patriotic sheriff was cast. Nothing came of his resistance, but in its spirit it is hard to see why it was less laudable than Hampden's contest against Ship-money, or than Hancock's audacity in having the Boston Custom-house officer locked up in

---

[1] *Cavendish Debates*, i. 442, with Mr. J. Wright's note.

the cabin of the *Liberty.* The King could never understand the prolonged fuss that was made about the
Middlesex election. "Nothing can be a greater proof
of a want of grievances," he wrote in 1773, "when
so trite an affair as the Middlesex election can be
hashed up every Session." [1] His zeal for the most
beautiful combination ever devised by man, as he
called the British Constitution, was not wholly according to knowledge.

In the same Parliament there was another and
scarcely less remarkable case of Privilege, "that eldest
son of Prerogative," as Burke truly called it, "and
inheriting all the vices of its parent." Certain printers
were accused of breach of privilege for reporting the
debates of the House (March, 1771). The messenger
of the serjeant-at-arms attempted to take one of them
into custody in his own shop in the City. A constable
was standing by, designedly, it has been supposed, and
Miller, the printer, gave the messenger into his custody
for an assault. The case came on before the Lord
Mayor, Alderman Wilkes, and Alderman Oliver, the
same evening, and the result was that the messenger of
the House was committed. The City doctrine was, that

[1] *Corr. with Lord North,* i. 131. Also at p. 233 (1775), he hopes
they have done with that "old bone of contention."

if the House of Commons had a serjeant-at-arms, they
had a serjeant-at-mace.   If the House of Commons
could send their citizens to Newgate, they could send
its messenger to the Compter.   Two other printers were
collusively arrested, brought before Wilkes and Oliver,
and at once liberated.   The King has had some credit
given him for warning Lord North to use every
caution to prevent this becoming a serious affair.
After all, the most stupid and pragmatic of beadles
generally learns by experience the wisdom of leaving
certain sorts of people to themselves.   But though
the King desired Lord North to be cautious, he had no
intention of letting the printers escape.   " Is not the
House of Lords, as a Court of Record," he asked, " the
best court to bring such miscreants [the printers]
before ? as it can fine as well as imprison, and as the
Lords have broader shoulders to support any odium
that this salutary measure may occasion in the minds
of the vulgar." [1]   By the vulgar, his Majesty as usual
meant the bulk of the people of England ; and by his
proposal to make the House of Lords a universal court
of first instance, for on no other theory could it take
any cognisance of a complaint of a breach of the

[1] Donne's *Correspondence of George III. with Lord North*, i. 57.

privileges of the Commons, he was endeavouring to set up an iniquitously unconstitutional doctrine. The design of this was clearly as unconstitutional as anything done in the Star Chamber. It is to be said that the Commons had been guilty of the same kind of offence against the laws in 1770, when they deliberately constituted themselves a court of justice, and *tried* Wilkes for his libel on Lord Weymouth, who was not a member of their House. The two cases were made still further to resemble one another by the fact that the Government had in the first instance brought Wilkes's libel forward as a breach of privilege, intending the Commons to decide in a matter affecting the privilege of the Lords, just as the King now thought it proper for the Lords to defend the privileges of the Commons.[1]

In the printers' matter, however, the Commons thought that their own shoulders were broad enough to bear any odium which a salutary measure might occasion in the minds of the vulgar—of the people, that is, whom they were supposed to represent. So the Lord Mayor and Alderman Oliver were sent to the Tower, where they lay until the prorogation of Parliament. Wilkes refused to pay any attention to repeated summonses to attend *at the bar* of the House, very

[1] See Massey's *History of England,* i. 273. (second ed.)

properly insisting that he ought to be summoned to attend *in his place* as member for Middlesex.[1] Besides committing Crosby and Oliver to the Tower, the House summoned the Lord Mayor's clerk to attend with his books, and then and there forced him to strike out the record of the recognisances into which their messenger had entered on being committed at the Mansion House. No Stuart ever did anything more arbitrary and illegal. The House deliberately intended to constitute itself, as Burke had said two years before, an arbitrary and despotic assembly. "The distempers of monarchy were the great subjects of apprehension and redress in the last century. In this, the distempers of Parliament."

So monstrous an interference with the records of an independent court, however, was only an incident in a

---

[1] In Sir T. May's otherwise excellent account of these transactions (*Constitutional Hist.* i. 427), he never mentions Wilkes without some evil epithet. He is "a dexterous and cunning agitator." The collision between the City and the House was mostly brought about by his "artful contrivances." His letter to the Speaker, declining to attend, was of a piece with his "usual effrontery." Now, even supposing Wilkes to have been rightfully deprived of his seat, and Sir T. May assuredly does not suppose this, Wilkes at least did not think so, and I don't see any effrontery in the fact of his refusing to allow by implication that he was not at this time the legal member for Middlesex. Very likely Wilkes was a bad man, but then bad men constantly do good things, and in a good way.

memorable struggle. It is an important illustration of the temper of the majority, but the significance of the contest lay in the violent repugnance of that majority to anything like the publication of their proceedings. Many years before this, Pulteney had declared that the publication of debates looked very like making them accountable without doors for what they said within, and this was exactly the issue in the present transactions. The majority of the House were as unwilling to admit their strict constitutional responsibility to the public as the Roman Senate or the Great Council. Their position was, on the whole, very much that of the King himself. I have already, at the beginning of the chapter, suggested reasons why this imitation was inevitable, or at least natural.

In one portion of the proceedings relative to the Middlesex election, Privilege and Prerogative had ominously stood side by side. When the London and Westminster petition, praying for a dissolution, and denouncing the arbitrary incapacitation of Wilkes, was presented to the King, a motion was passed in the House that the allegations in the Remonstrance were unwarrantable, tending to destroy the allegiance of the subject, by withdrawing him from obedience to the laws (March, 1770). The Remonstrants had boldly, and not more boldly than truly, set forth that "there is a time when it is morally demonstrable that men cease to be representatives. That time is now arrived. The House of Commons do not represent the people."

Lord Chatham, in his place in the House of Lords, had declared the same thing. "The Commons," he said, "have betrayed their constituents, and violated the constitution." "What is this mysterious power," he went on to ask, "undefined by law, unknown to the subject, which we must not approach without awe, nor speak of without reverence—which no man may question, and to which all men must submit? My Lords, I thought the slavish doctrine of passive obedience had long since been exploded; and when our kings were obliged to confess that their title to the crown and the rule of their government had no other foundation than the known laws of the land/I never expected to hear a Divine right or a Divine infallibility attributed to any other branch of the legislature." But the pretensions of the Lower House were nothing less than this. In some respects they were even more than royal. In 1774, for instance, a libel on the Speaker appeared in the *Public Advertiser.* It was properly suggested that Sir Fletcher Norton should be left to the remedy of a lawsuit. "What," cried Charles Fox, then, as even in 1782, a staunch upholder of Privilege, " was *any member*, much less the Speaker, to be grossly assailed and left to a lawsuit for a remedy ?   It would be no less absurd for the House to appeal to an inferior court, than for the Court of King's Bench to apply for protection to the Court of Common Pleas."   Did Fox remember that the sovereign himself is obliged thus to appeal to an inferior court ?   Still the bulk of the members, in these bad times, as on many previous occasions,[1] and on some since, could not divest themselves of the idea that the House is a court of law.   The mischief flowing from such a doctrine is very obvious.   The public liberties were in as much peril from these arbitrary assumptions of an oligarchic chamber, as they had ever been in from the arbitrary assumptions of an unconstitutional sovereign.   Traditions of the supreme authority of the Lower House were rapidly crystallising into a form that was wholly incompatible with anything like free government.

As is usual when the minds of those in power have been infected with this arbitrary temper, the employment of military force to repress civil disturbances became a familiar and favourite idea.   The military,

[1] See Hallam's *Constitutional History*, c. xvi. sect. iii.

said Lord Weymouth, in his famous letter to the Surrey magistrates, *"can never be employed to a more constitutional purpose than in the support of the authority and dignity of the magistracy."* If the magistrate should be menaced, "he is cautioned not to delay a moment in calling for the aid of the military, and making use of them effectually." Such an occasion "always presents itself when the civil power is trifled with and insulted." The consequence of this bloody scroll, as Wilkes rightly called it, was that shortly afterwards an affray occurred between the crowd and the troops, in which some twenty people were killed and wounded (May 10, 1768). Instead of keeping the military in the background until absolutely wanted, the magistrates, along with the soldiers, at once came upon the ground. The following day, the Secretary of War, Lord Barrington, wrote to the commanding officer, informing him that "his Majesty highly approves of the conduct both of officers and men, and means that his gracious approbation of them should be communicated to them by you." "I beg you will be pleased to assure them that every possible regard shall be shown to them. Their zeal and good behaviour on this occasion deserve it; and *in case any disagreeable circumstance should happen in the execution of their duty, they shall have every defence and protection that the law can authorise and that this office can give."* This gracious approval of bloodshed, and encouraging invitation to shed more blood whenever an opportunity should offer, needs no comment. It is worth remembering as a set-off, when one hears people talking nonsense about King George's honesty and sincerity, just as if sincerity were any palliative in a ruler for folly, incompetence, and a savage's indifference to human life.[1] Various other steps were taken to show that Lord Barrington had promised not a word more than he meant to perform.

Burke brought the matter before the House in a motion for a Committee of Inquiry, supported by one of the most lucid and able of his minor speeches. "If ever the time should come," he concluded, "when this House shall be found prompt to execute and slow to inquire ; ready to punish the excesses of the people, and slow to listen to their grievances ; ready to grant supplies, and slow to examine the account ; ready to

---

[1] The complacency with which he contemplated the time "when decrepitude or death should put an end to" Lord Chatham, is familiar. (*Corr. with Lord North*, i. 261). Yet, "I am not conscious of having much gall in my composition" (i. 71). There is a ghastly kind of quaintness in the ease with which he looks out for windfalls in the way of patronage, and expresses his conviction first that one and then another cannot "last long."

invest magistrates with large powers, and slow to inquire into the exercise of them ; ready to entertain notions of the military power as incorporated with the constitution,—when you learn this in the air of St. James's, then the business is done ; then the House of Commons will change that character which it receives from the people only." Of course his motion for a committee was lost by an enormous and overwhelming majority.[1]

Another transaction which befell in the same Parliament may be cited to show the evil courses on which the majority in the House were firmly set. In 1769 the minister came down with the information that his Majesty had got rather more than half a million into debt, and that he relied on " the known zeal and affection of his faithful Commons, that they would make provision for enabling his Majesty to discharge the same." Manifestly nobody was likely to oppose the making of such a provision. Not even the democratic aldermen, Beckford and Trecothick, who opened the discussion upon the message, hinted that they would like the court tradesmen to become bankrupt, or the foreign ministers to go unpaid, through the scandalous insolvency of the monarch. But, on the other hand,

[1] **245 against 30.** *Cavendish Debates,* i. 307—337.

no legislator with the dimmest conception of duty to the nation would have dreamt of instantly complying with the demands of the royal bankrupt, before the production and examination of the accounts. Duty to the nation, however, was not a generally esteemed sentiment. The accounts were not allowed to be produced. " Let us relieve the Crown," Lord North cried, " as we ought, wisely, frankly, cheerfully, dutifully." Dutifulness to the Crown overruled all meaner motives, and half a million of the public money went in channels that were never disclosed to the public eye. Taxpayers might have been pardoned if they had failed to see any difference between their own position and that of their ancestors who had been made blindly to pay Ship-money and Benevolences, except the unimportant point that the House of Commons was now the facile instrument through which the sovereign reached them. The extortion was more decorously managed in the days of George III. than in those of Charles I., but the principle, that the public should pay money for royal purposes which they had no chance of scrutinising or controlling, was identical. The great and ever - memorable illustration and overthrow of this principle was still to come.[1]

---

[1] The debates on the Civil List Arrears, in Cavendish (i. 268—306),

are

It is a relief to turn from the contemplation of these
narrow, selfish, and slavish ideas, to those other loftier,
wider, and more enduring views of the function of the
Lower House in Government, of which Burke was the
wise and passionate champion.   He at least never
yielded to "that indifference to the constitution which
had been for some time growing among our gentry." [1]
He was not absolutely insensible to the fatal splendour
of the theory of a patriot king.   "A system unfavourable to freedom may be so formed as considerably to
exalt the grandeur of the State ; and men may find in
the pride and splendour of that prosperity some sort

are very full and very interesting.   See also *Present Discontents*,
Works, i. 145.   In 1769 a debt of £513,000 was paid for the Civil
List ; in 1777 a debt of £618,340 (besides the addition of another
hundred thousand a year to the Civil List) ; in 1786, a debt of
£210,000 ; and so on until the end of the reign, when it was found
that " the several arrears paid off by Parliament, exclusive of the debt
of £300,000 charged on the Civil List in 1782, amounted to £3,398,000."
(May's *Const. History*, i. 206.)   The nation, however, was only too
proud to pay handsomely in this and a good many other ways, for the
majestic and heroic virtues of a ruler who would dine, as Adding-
ton testifies, on chops and a dumpling, and who abstained from
debauching the maids of honour.   A careful comparison of the financial atrocities of this reign with the thrift of such a man as Frederick
the Great is painfully instructive.   But England, as Mr. Carlyle says,
was the inventor of " that sublime art of rolling over on you know not
whom the expenditure, needful or needless, of your heavy-laden self."
  [1] *Present Discontents*, Works, i. 133, *b.*

of consolation for the loss of their solid privileges."
But the system which it was then being attempted to
impose tended to produce " neither the security of a
free government nor the energy of a monarchy that
is absolute." [1]   Political force was not drawn either
from the concentrated vigour of a single indomitable
and unfettered will, nor from the tidal impulses and
passions of a whole nation.   Everything that was
done was done in an indirect, underhand, and complex
way. The King had to manage the ministers.   The
ministers and the King together had to manage the
House.   The House thus managed was indifferent alike
to the wishes and welfare of those for whom it was
the appointed guardian and trustee.   Well might Chatham declare, Before the end of this century either
the Parliament will reform itself from within, or be
reformed with a vengeance from without.

Burke was uniformly consistent in his view of the
remedies which the various sections of Opposition
proposed against the existing debasement and servility
of the Lower House.   The Duke of Richmond wanted
universal suffrage, equal electoral districts, and annual
parliaments.   Wilkes—perhaps I ought to add, in
the conventional manner, with his usual effrontery—

[1] Ibid. 136, *b*.

proposed to disfranchise the rotten boroughs, to increase the county constituencies, and to give members to rich, populous, trading towns, — a general policy which was accepted fifty-six years afterwards. The Constitutional Society desired frequent parliaments, the exclusion of placemen from the House, and the increase of the county representation.[1] Burke uniformly refused to give his countenance to any proposals, such as these, which involved a clearly organic change in the constitution. He confessed that he had no sort of reliance upon either a triennial parliament or a place-bill, and with that reasonableness which as a rule was fully as remarkable in him as his eloquence, he showed very good grounds for his want of faith in the popular specifics.[2] An election, he argued, is a contest between independent gentlemen and the Treasury. The more often the election comes, the greater the strain upon the resources of the candidate. It is easy to see which of the contending parties would be

---

[1] The Constitutional Society was founded after the Society for the Support of the Bill of Rights had been destroyed by the rupture between Horne and Wilkes. The Wilkites were excluded from the composition of the Constitutional Society.

[2] Junius was for triennial parliaments, and this of itself would be enough to overthrow the hypothesis that Burke and Junius were one. See Cooke's *Hist. of Party*, iii. 133.

ruined first. Everybody, he said, must have noticed
how prodigiously greater the power of ministry is in
the first and last session of a parliament than it is
in the intermediate periods, when members sit a little
firm in their seats. The thing to be desired, then, was
the diminution of the Government influence in elections ; and how was this end furthered by the mere
multiplication of elections ? " About the close of the
last Parliament and the beginning of this, several agents
for boroughs went about, and I remember well that it
was in every one of their mouths, ' Sir, your election
will cost you £3,000, if you are independent ; but if
the Ministry supports you, it may be done for two, and
perhaps for less ;' and indeed the thing spoke for itself.
When a living was to be got for one, a commission in
the army for another, a lift in the navy for a third, and
Custom-house offices scattered about without measure
or number, who doubts but money may be saved ? A
gentlemen of £2,000 a year, who meets another of the
same fortune, fights with equal arms ; but if to one of
the candidates you add a thousand a year in places
for himself, and a power of giving away as much among
others, one must, or there is no truth in arithmetical
demonstration, ruin his adversary if he is to meet him
and to fight with him every third year." Besides tear-

ing to pieces the fortunes of independent men, frequency of election would make the whole body of the people " more lawless, more idle, more debauched" it would utterly destroy the sobriety, the industry, the integrity, the simplicity of all the people." " Their heads will never cool; the temptations of elections will be for ever glittering before their eyes. They will all grow politicians; every one, quitting his business, will choose to enrich himself by his vote; they will take the gauging rod; new places will be made for them; they will run to the Custom-house quay; their looms and ploughs will be deserted." And at length, " I do not seriously think this constitution, even to the wrecks of it, could survive five triennial elections." [1]

The wildness of this sudden exaggeration in the midst of such solid and reasonable argument is intensely Burkian. There can, however, be no doubt that the frequent recurrence of elections in America has been attended by some of the disadvantages which Burke apprehended. And triennial or annual parliaments could have done no good, unless it had been accompanied by the more important process of " amputating," as Chatham called it, the rotten boroughs, of

---

[1] *Speech on a Bill for Shortening the Duration of Parliaments,* Works, ii. 483, *b*; *Appeal from New to Old Whigs,* Works, i. 502.

which it is calculated that at this time the Crown could reckon some seventy as its own property. Besides those which belonged to the Crown, there was also the immense number which belonged more or less directly to the Peerage. If the King wanted to strengthen an administration the thing needful was not to enlist the services of able and distinguished men, but to conciliate a duke. The support of the duke and of his major and minor satellites in the Upper House brought with it the control of a given quantity of voting power in the Lower House. If the administration had only dukes enough, a majority in the Commons was assured. The only possible way, for example, of enabling the youthful Pitt to keep his head above water was to give him a cabinet in which he was the solitary commoner.[1] All this patrician influence, which may be found at the bottom of most of the intrigues of the reign, operated with the pocket boroughs for instruments. The rottenness of the rotten boroughs would not have been touched by curtailing the duration of Parliaments.

Nothing, again, can be more rational and well-con-

---

[1] In the Cabinet which Pitt formed on his second accession to office, in 1804, he and Castlereagh were the only two Commoners out of twelve persons. His first Cabinet only contained seven persons, so that the proportion of peers was not much altered.

sidered than the line of argument by which he depre-
cates the proposals for excluding from the House all
placemen and pensioners upon the Crown. Is it not
better, he asked, that the greater part of those who hold
civil employments, and of such mighty and important
bodies as the military and naval establishments, should
have even a corrupt interest in the forms of the constitution, than that they should have none at all?
Again, if the Government were deprived of this open
and avowed sort of influence, would they not be sure
at once to resort to oblique and underhand ways?
" For," he added, with one of those incomparably
luminous and profound strokes that are not absent
even in his most extravagant sallies, *it is no incon-
siderable part of wisdom to know how much of an evil
ought to be tolerated,* lest by attempting a degree of
purity impracticable in degenerate times and manners,
instead of cutting off the subsisting ill practices, new
corruptions might be introduced for the concealment
and security of the old." Of all the modes of influence, a place openly held under the Government
appeared to him the least discreditable to the man who
holds it, and by far the least dangerous to the national
interests.

What, then, was the remedy, or was there no remedy

for these grave distempers of Parliament? Only the remedy of the interposition of the body of the people itself. We must beware of interpreting this phrase in the modern democratic sense. The central article of the democratic faith, its cardinal dogma, is that a depth and a strength of virtue and power is developed in the massing and union of men, which is no more to be measured by the force of the individual, than the might of the waves of the sea is to be measured by the tiny salt pools on the sand. This conception, though destined to leaven and convert prevailing political ideas into their most effective future forms, was barely, if at all, realised in England at this time, and by Burke least of all men. In 1766 he had deliberately declared that he thought it would be more conformable to the spirit of the constitution, by lessening the number, to add to the weight and independency of our voters." Considering the immense and dangerous charge of elections, the prostitute and daring venality, the corruption of manners, the idleness and profligacy of the lower sort of voters, no prudent man would propose to increase such an evil." [1] In another place he denies that the people have either enough of speculation in the closet or of experience

---

[1] *Observations on late State of the Nation*, Works, i. 105, *b.*

in business, to be competent judges, not of the detail of particular measures only, but of *general schemes of policy* [1]—the assumption on which the Whig or Benevolent Aristocratic theory has been uniformly made to rest. Even in the circumstances of the election of 1774, when the Opposition candidates were pressed to pledge themselves to support a given set of instructions, and when Burke might perhaps have been excused for some sort of compliance, he declined point-blank to go to Westminster as a Bristol delegate. It is the duty of a representative, he said to the people who had just elected him, to sacrifice his repose and his pleasure to his constituents ; and, above all, ever, and in all cases, to prefer their *interest* to his own. His judgment, on the contrary, he ought never under any circumstances to sacrifice. " Your representative owes you not his industry only, but his judgment ; and he betrays, instead of serving you, if he sacrifices it to your opinion." [2] On Burke's theory, the people, as a rule, were no more concerned to interfere with Parliament than a man is concerned to interfere with somebody whom he has voluntarily and deliberately made his trustee. But here, he confessed, was a

[1] *Speech on Duration of Parliaments,* Works, ii. 482, *b.*
[2] *Speech at Conclusion of the Poll,* Ibid. i. 179, *b.*

shameful and ruinous breach of trust. The ordinary rule of government was being every day mischievously contemned and daringly set aside. Until the confidence thus outraged should be once more restored, then the people ought to be excited to a more strict and detailed attention to the conduct of their representatives. First, the meetings of counties and corporations ought to settle standards for judging more systematically of the behaviour of those whom they had sent to Parliament. Secondly, frequent and correct lists of the voters in all important questions ought to be procured. Thirdly, the severest discouragement ought to be given to the pernicious practice of affording a blind and undistinguishing support to every administration. "Parliamentary support comes and goes with office, totally regardless of the man or the merit."[1] The

---

[1] For instance, Wilkes's annual motion to expunge the votes upon the Middlesex election had been uniformly rejected as often as it was made while Lord North was in power. Lord North had no sooner given way to the Rockingham Cabinet than the House of Commons changed its mind, and the resolutions were expunged, by a handsome majority of 115 to 47.

In 1779-80, when Lord Thurlow was, by the King's commands, endeavouring to strengthen administration by securing the accession of some of the Opposition, he complained that Lord North looked too exclusively and simply to the concurrence of members of Parliament. "In my notion," said Thurlow, "the strength of a ministry consists, besides the credit and esteem of Parliament, in their influence upon

will of the King was omnipotent over his ministers, because he would endure none for ministers who would not brook his omnipotence. And administration was omnipotent in the House, because, as we have seen, it could be a man's most efficient friend at an election, and could most amply reward his fidelity afterwards. Against this system Burke called on the nation to set a stern face. Root it up, he kept crying; settle the general course in which you desire members to go; insist that they shall not suffer themselves to be diverted from this by the authority of the government of the day; let lists of votes be published, so that you may ascertain for yourselves whether your trustees have been faithful or fraudulent; do all this, and there will be no need to resort to those organic changes, those empirical innovations, which may possibly cure, but are much more likely to destroy.[1]

It is not surprising that so halting a policy should have given deep displeasure to very many, perhaps to most, of those whose only common bond

other parts of the empire, and other great bodies within the kingdom; their authority over the fleets and armies, and other branches of executive government, together with many other obvious articles." Cf. Donne's *Correspondence of George III. with Lord North*, ii. 301.

[1] *Present Discontents*, Works, i. 147, *a*; 149, *b*.

was the loose and negative sentiment of antipathy to the Court, the ministry, and the too servile majority of the House of Commons. The Constitutional Society was furious. Lord Chatham wrote to Lord Rockingham that the work in which these doctrines first appeared must do much mischief to the common cause. And the extreme advanced party was probably right, as extreme advanced parties are usually found to have been, by the time they have persuaded their more timorous neighbours to join them. Their policy was revolutionary, it is true, but in estimating the precise amount of evil which it may be proper to associate with the idea of revolution, we ought fairly to remember what overtook the nation in its stead.

Between the publication of Burke's *Thoughts on the Discontents* and the retirement of the King, there was an interval of about forty years. Deduct from this the ten years of Pitt's peace administration, and the rest is the history of prolonged, arbitrary, and violent repression, first in the colonies and afterwards at home. After 1794 the system of government was simply one of absolute despotism. A careful study of the repressive and tyrannical proceedings of this long epoch must convince anybody with an open mind that no subversion of the constitution at the hands of red

I

democrats could possibly have been more complete
than that which, by the end of the eighteenth century,
had been effected by the oligarchs.   The Constitutional
Society in the end was fully justified by the disasters
of despotism in being willing to face the dangers of
democracy.   Burke, however, thought otherwise, as he
thought twenty years afterwards.

"Our constitution," in his opinion, "stands on a
nice equipoise, with steep precipices and deep waters
upon all sides of it.   In removing it from a dangerous
leaning towards one side, there may be a risk of over-
setting it on the other."[1]   This image was ever before
his mind.   It occurs again in the last sentence of that
great protest against all change and movement, when
he describes himself as one who, "when the equipoise
of the vessel in which he sails may be endangered by
overloading it upon one side, is desirous of carrying
the small weight of his reasons to that which may
preserve its equipoise."[2]   Yet, could the most bitter
despiser of the constitution have devised a more
damaging metaphor?   The constitution is no vast and
imposing structure, with foundations laid deep, strong,
and wide in the energy, enlightenment, integrity, and

[1] *Present Discontents*, Works, i. 148, *a.*
[2] *Reflections*, Ibid. i. 475, *b.*

reparative vigour of those for whom the structure was raised and for whom it exists. It is a thing standing on a nice equipoise; any trifling displacement of a stone or a beam may serve to topple it over the steep precipices and down into the deep waters which encircle it on all sides. If this were so, what could its best friend more strenuously desire than that it should be removed with all convenient speed from so perilous an elevation, and placed in unshaken security upon the plain? Burke's theory, which is the Whig and oligarchic theory at its best, implies a forgetfulness of the great truth that there is a kind of natural health in the body politic as in the body physical, by which only a sound existence and a robust vitality can be hoped to be made to continue. His theory attributes too much importance to outward gear and wrappages. These are, indeed, useful or indispensable. But the nice apprehensions of Burke, the timorous cautions of the men who insist on a multiplicity of checks and balances, involve the evil paradox that health depends less upon inborn vigour and force than upon, not merely the quality of the material, but the precise cut and fashion of the political vestment. An inch more here or an inch less there, an extra fold or a fold the fewer, an additional trimming in one place or a seam

or a band in another place—these are the salvation
or the ruin of the wearer.

In spite of his disbelief in specifics for political
distempers, Burke had bewailed the loss of the practice of impeachment, as the sacrifice of "that great
guardian of the purity of the constitution."[1] The
decay of this idea might have roused him to see that
less depends upon institutions than upon the spirit
which gives to them their vitality. The very circumstances which made the necessity of impeachment so
extreme and urgent were precisely those which inevitably prevented the employment of that remedy,
and in fact took it out of the list of remedies, even
to the idea of it. What are we to think of a safe-
guard which ceases to operate just when the need for
it has grown strongest? While the constitution is
pure, while the House of Commons is vigilant and
patriotic enough to impeach a bad minister, and the
House of Lords firm enough to convict him, the safe-
guard is worthy of its name. But the conditions
which clogged up the legislative and executive parts
of the constitution, inevitably and at the very same
time clogged up its corrective parts also. And this
must always be the case. A constitution is only a

[1] *Present Discontents,* Works, i. 141.

machine. A thorough derangement of the fundamental structure throws no less thoroughly out of gear all the ingenious contrivances which suffice excellently well for minor irregularities. What is gained by pointing to clever safety-valves, and infallible guiding rods, and unerring steam-gauges, when there is no steam being forced in, and the whole machine is choked and corroded with rust? " We Englishmen," Burke once said, complacently, " stop very short of the principles upon which we support any given part of our constitution, or even the whole of it together." [1] True, and we are wise in so doing, provided only the working result of this accommodation of first principles to practical conditions is, in all its aspects, decently satisfactory. It is clearly in the nature of this, as of all similar accommodations, to need revision. The practical conditions change. The working result is decently satisfactory no more. Surely at this point, to boast of stopping very short of the principles of the constitution is fatuous and disgraceful. If the principles have that elasticity and flexibility which should belong to them, it is to them that we shall best recur in search of fresh and more powerful springs of political action. There may be no harm in partially

Speech on Conciliation with America, Works, i. 200, *b.*

damming up the water sources when otherwise they might flood the plain; but when everything is parched and withered, when the peril is of an opposite kind, what can be more untimeous and ill-omened than to persist in keeping the wells sealed up, and in refusing to widen and multiply the conduits?

In that fine and exhaustive piece of reasoning, the *Speech on American Taxation,* the orator reproaches George Grenville for "thinking better of the wisdom and power of human legislation than in truth it deserves. . . . He conceived," Burke continues, "and many conceived along with him, that the flourishing trade of this country was greatly owing to law and institution, and not quite so much to liberty; for but too many are apt to believe regulation to be commerce, and taxes to be revenue." Grenville was for diligently enforcing the Navigation Laws against the American traders, thinking that the size of the trade and the prosperity which it brought alike to the colonies and to the mother country, were the fruit of legal restrictions rather than of the energetic and enterprising spirit which animated the merchants. Was this very dissimilar from Burke's own mistake, which attributed the origin and secret of liberty itself to institutions that were only possible where liberty had been before?

If Grenville mistook regulation for commerce and taxation for revenue, did not Burke go too near confounding the mechanism of liberty with its spirit and ultimate source of momentum ? Does he ever speak of the constitution—and let us remember what it was in his day—without falling into a fallacy identical with that which he himself described and denounced as thinking better of the wisdom and power of human legislation than in truth it deserves ?

"Our constitution," he cried, in an oration against parliamentary reform, "is like an island which uses and restrains its subject sea; in vain the waves roar. In that constitution I know, and exultingly I feel, both that I am free and that I am not free dangerously to myself or to others."[1] It was under this constitution that the Middlesex electors had been robbed for six years of what was as much their own as the freeholds

---

[1] *Speech on a Motion* (1782) *for a Committee to inquire into the State of the Representation of the Commons in Parliament,* Works, ii. 489, a. In this speech, among other things, Burke fell into the fallacy, so often repeated in later days, of maintaining that unrepresented places had nothing to complain of, after all, because the members for the places that were represented were equally interested in the prosperity of the whole. "Warwick has members ; is Warwick or Stafford more happy, opulent, or free than Newcastle or than Birmingham? Is Wiltshire the pampered favourite, whilst Yorkshire, like the child of the bond-woman, is turned out to the desert ?"

in virtue of which they went through the empty formality of voting; that Mansfield's pestilent doctrine of
libel being a matter for judges and not for juries to
decide, had been allowed to stand; that taxes had been
recklessly and perversely sanctioned upon the unrepresented colonies : and it was under this constitution
that in later days every enormity was perpetrated
against public freedom that a Bourbon or a Stuart
could have sighed for.[1] Burke might know that he
was free in 1782. People knew that they were not
free twelve years before, and they knew it again
twelve years later. Wilkes did not feel Burke's proud
and comfortable sentiment of freedom when he was
carried to prison on a general warrant; nor the
colonists when they were asked to pay stamp duty;
nor did any living Englishman in that reign of terror
which began in this country with the outbreak of the
crusade against the French Republic. The history of
the English constitution over the whole period of
Burke's career, and some years after death had silenced
his panegyrics, is the history of about the most in-

---

[1] Take, for instance, 36 George III. c. 8, and 39 George III. c. 79.
Lord Campbell, no violent writer, allows that in 1794 the alternative
seemed to be servitude or civil war. Fox, Sheridan, and Grey openly
averred in 1795 that they thought resistance to the laws was justified,
if it could be proved likely to succeed.

adequate and mischievous set of political arrangements that any country has ever yet had to endure. Yet it was this which Burke declared that he looked upon with filial reverence. " Never will I cut it in pieces, and put it into the kettle of any magician, in order to boil it with the puddle of their compounds into youth and vigour ; on the contrary, I will drive away such pretenders ; I will nurse its venerable age, and with lenient arts extend a parent's breath." [1]

He was filled with the spirit, and he borrowed the arguments, which have always marked the champion of faith and authority against the impious assault of reason or innovation. The constitution was sacred to him as the voice of the Church, and the oracles of her saints are sacred to the believer. Study it, he cried, until you know how to admire it, and if you cannot know and admire, rather believe that you are dull than that the rest of the world has been imposed upon. We ought to understand it according to our measure, and to venerate where we are not able

---

[1] Works, ii. 490, *b*. Sheridan, writing of a debate on Sawbridge's motion in 1782 : " Burke acquitted himself with the most magnanimous indiscretion, attacked William Pitt in a scream of passion, and swore Parliament was, and always had been, precisely what it ought to be, and that all people who thought of reforming it wanted to overturn the Constitution." Quoted in Earl Stanhope's *Life of Pitt*, i. 76.

presently to comprehend.[1]   Well has Burke been called the Bossuet of politics.

Although, however, Burke's unflinching reverence for the constitution, and his reluctance to lay a finger upon it, may now seem clearly excessive, as it did to Chatham and his son, who were great men in the right, or to Beckford and Sawbridge, who were very little men in the right, we can only be just to him by comparing his ideas with those which were dominant throughout this evil reign.   While he opposed more frequent parliaments, he still upheld the doctrine that " to govern according to the sense and agreeably to the interests of the people is a great and glorious object of government."   While he declared himself against the addition of a hundred knights of the shire, he in the very same breath protested that, though the people might be deceived in their choice of an object, he " could scarcely conceive any choice they could make to be so very mischievous as the existence of any human force capable of resisting it."[2]   To us this may seem very mild and commonplace doctrine, but it was not commonplace in an age when Anglican

[1] Works, i. 536, *a.*
[2] *To the Chairman of the Buckinghamshire Meeting,* 1780, Works, ii. 430, *a.*

divines—men like Archbishop Markham, Dr. Nowell or Dr. Porteous—had revived the base precepts of passive obedience and non-resistance, and when such a man as Lord Mansfield encouraged them. And these were the kind of foundations which Burke had been laying while Fox was yet a Tory, while Sheridan was writing farces, and while Grey was a schoolboy. The political husbandman does not always foresee what manner of crop will be gathered from off the lands that he has digged and sown.

It is, however, almost demonstrably certain that the vindication of the supremacy of popular interests over all other considerations would have been bootless toil, and that the great constitutional struggle from 1760 to 1783 would have ended otherwise than it did, but for the failure of the war against the insurgent colonies, and the final establishment of American Independence. It was this portentous transaction which finally routed the arbitrary and despotic pretensions of the House of Commons[1] over the people, which put an end to the hopes entertained by the sovereign of making

---

[1] See Sir G. C. Lewis's *Administrations of Great Britain*, p. 28. "The House had now proved," Fox said on the evening of North's resignation, "their abhorrence of a government of influence; the new ministers must ever bear in mind that fact, and remember that to the House they owed their situations."

his personal will supreme in the Chambers, and which
established the principle of Cabinet as distinguished
from departmental responsibility.   Fox might well talk
of an early Royalist victory in the war as the terrible
news from Long Island.   The struggle which began
unsuccessfully at Brentford in Middlesex, was continued at Boston in Massachusetts.   The scene had
changed, but the conflicting principles were the same.
The defeat and subjugation of the colonists would
have been followed by the final annihilation of the
Opposition in the mother country.   The war of Independence was virtually a second English civil war.
The ruin of the American cause would have been also
the ruin of the constitutional cause in England; and
a patriotic Englishman may revere the memory of
Patrick Henry and George Washington not less justly
than the patriotic American.   Burke's attitude in this
great contest is that part of his history about the
majestic and noble wisdom of which there can be least
dispute.

CHAPTER IV.

A T the Peace of 1763, more than one shrewd contemporary pointed out what he conceived to be the folly of the English Government in choosing to retain Canada instead of some of the islands of which they had gained possession during the war. With the French on their borders, it was argued, the colonists would have had their attachment to the mother country constantly stimulated by apprehension and jealousy of their foreign neighbours. The close proximity of an encroaching power would have kept them as steady in their allegiance to England as they had shown themselves in the face of French encroachments in former times. From this point of view, it might be held that one of the first results of Pitt's triumphant colonial war was the loss of the greatest colonies of all.

But it is impossible for any one who has studied the elements which composed the character of the

rebellious colonists to believe that the transformation
of Canada into an English dependency was at all an
essential or indispensable condition of a rupture with
the mother country. It was, perhaps, a favourable
accident. It removed a slender obstruction, which
might have interposed a very slight delay. It made
the growth of the idea of rebellion in the minds of
the colonists a shade more unimpeded than it might
have been otherwise. But the roots of the idea were
there already, full of life and vigour. Whether the
French had remained possessors of Canada or not, the
first deliberate attempt at oppression on the part of
the mother country was sure to kindle resistance.
Long before the expulsion of the French, the notion
of taxing the colonists had been suggested to Walpole,
but that profoundly sagacious man promptly rejected
so perilous a scheme. The project was just as dangerous in his day as it proved to be when its execution
was actually attempted.

There was another prophecy made upon the settlement of Canada. In that settlement the Government
left the Catholic population, numbering 150,000 against
less than 400 Protestants, in the full enjoyment of
their privileges. It was foretold at the time,—as
Burke did not forget twenty years later, when arguing

for concessions to another Catholic population, four times as large as its Protestant oppressors,—" that the Pope would send his indulgences thither; that the Canadians would fall in with France; would declare independence, and draw or force our colonies into the same design. The independence happened according to this prediction, but in directly the reverse order. All our English Protestant countries revolted. They joined themselves to France; and it so happened that popish Canada was the only place which preserved its fidelity. Vain," he well concludes, " vain are all the prognostics taken from ideas and passions which survive the state of things that gave rise to them." [1]

Independence was the grand root from which the old colonies had sprung. It was their most ancient tradition. The Puritans, out of whose loins the chiefs of the rebellious colonists had come, began by throwing off the yoke of authority, whether it was embodied in the traditions of an invisible and eternal Church, or in the less mystic form of a dignified hierarchy. It is true that they soon forgot their own principle, imposed illogical restrictions on their own doctrines, and applied themselves to the organization of an authority not less arbitrary and oppressive than that of Bonner or of

[1] *Letter to Sir Hercules Langrishe*, Works, i. 560, *a.*

Laud. Some episodes in the history of Puritanism in America are at least as revolting as any of the crimes which interested polemists are accustomed to lay at the door of Catholicism or Anglicanism in England. But the principle of a system continues to work apart from temporary distortions and perversions. The Puritans might forget for a time that they owed their very existence to the vindication of the right of free judgment. Still, the old tradition of throwing off the episcopal yoke survived through all this to colour their lives and opinions. Their disrespect for human authority in theology led by a natural association of ideas to a no less warm disapproval of arbitrary authority in the political sphere. This connexion was inevitable.

The revolutionary power latent in the Protestant doctrine was shown in the daring and unparalleled revolt of the Dutch against Philip II. in the sixteenth century. If we take into account the thoroughness with which the notion of respect for temporal authority had incorporated itself with the European life of that time, if we realize fully the awful divinity which then did hedge a king, we shall be able to appreciate the forces inherent in a theory which could animate a people,—after long and horrible sufferings, it is true,—with moral daring enough to scatter these venerated traditions to the winds.

In England in the seventeenth century, the social conditions were not ripe for the general movement to which the Puritan sentiment, thus expanded and transformed, seemed clearly to point. The preparation of public opinion was incomplete. The intellectual basis of anti-aristocratic ideas had not yet been sufficiently strongly laid. The policy which had suppressed the House of Lords was prematurely enlightened. There had been no Eighteenth Century, and the critical doctrine was still in its initial phase. It was impossible permanently to revolutionize an old society with deep and twisted roots, by such imperfectly tempered weapons as Puritanism was able to furnish out of its armoury. Cromwell's native ascendancy of character compensated for this imperfection while he remained to guide the course of affairs. At his death the current of social conditions, which had only been dammed up, and not finally diverted into new channels, flowed on in its old bed with only a slightly accelerated rapidity. In the colonies the case was widely different. The Puritan idea, alike in its own theological order and in the political order where it had struck a firm root, was checked by no encounter with an old social state too

K

deeply laid to be speedily modified. The colonies offered an open field for its free spread and unrestrained development. Feudalism had never been transplanted, for hereditary privilege and the multiform ideas which spring from the legal recognition of primogeniture,[1] were too exclusively the products of European development to bear removal into a strange and keener air. There was no Church in alliance with a territorial aristocracy, ready to purchase the patronage of the State by the degrading advocacy of absolutist principles, eager by the dissemination of despotic doctrine to earn deaneries and bishoprics. Thus the lapse of a century and a half gave time for the spirit of independence to grow ineradicably into the national character. / The American Rebellion was the third and last illustration of the regenerative force of Protestantism. / The Dutch Revolt and the English Civil War had been more religious than political. The third was political in form and in substance, but its impulses and momentum came from the distant struggle of old days for the right of private judgment. For the third and last time the wave of Protestantism swept forward and submerged a political system.[2]

---

[1] The Cavalier colony of Virginia was in this point an exception.

[2] "All Protestantism, even the most cold and passive, is a sort of

The forms and ceremonial of government in an old country have clustering round them innumerable associations which cannot be suddenly touched without subverting order and dissolving society. In the colonies, the special forms of government were no more than an external accident. Those powerful associations which lie half-concealed about the roots and foundations of national character were in the minds of the colonists rather inclined in the direction of resistance than of reverence. This was their inherited predisposition. Their ancestors had resisted the arbitrary designs of a monarch in the seventeenth century, and had only partially succeeded, because the

dissent. But the religion most prevalent in our northern colonies is a refinement on the principle of resistance ; it is the dissidence of dissent, and the protestantism of the Protestant religion. This religion, under a variety of denominations agreeing in nothing but in the communion of the spirit of liberty, is predominant in most of the northern provinces, where the Church of England, notwithstanding its legal rights, is in reality no more than a sort of private sect, not comprising, most probably, the tenth of the people. The colonists left England when this spirit was high, and in the emigrants was highest of all ; and even that stream of foreigners which has been constantly flowing into these colonies has, for the greatest part, been composed of dissenters from the establishments of their several countries, and have brought with them a temper and character far from alien to that of the people with whom they mixed."—*Speech on Conciliation with America*, Works, i. 187, *b*. Cf. also Comte's *Positive Philosophy* (English Translation), ii. 341.

social conditions of old establishment were much too strong for them. In the eighteenth century arbitrary pretensions had sprung up in the Imperial Parliament. The colonists were as resolute in resisting the unconstitutional claims of Lord North's majority as their forefathers had been in withstanding the claims of Charles I. ⌈The great American rebellion of the eighteenth century was the sequel of the great English rebellion of the seventeenth century.⌋ Fortunately, in America no barrier of time-honoured loyalty, of timorous adherence to ideas which had become too narrow to meet the facts, obstructed the prosperous course of the revolution. With admirable promptitude, as soon as ever the struggle became unmistakeable and unavoidable, the colonists at the very outset took up the ground which they finally maintained in triumph. There never was a revolution on the whole—and I do not forget the winter of 1779–80—so little stayed and fretted by doubters and Laodiceans, by quaking hair-splitters and moon-struck refiners. The leaders of the rebellion were able to take this decisive and unhesitating stand, without pausing in prolonged and unprofitable debate, as a consequence of that fermentation of free ideas which had been in process among them ever since the birth of the colonies. As

there had never been any ancient and venerable attachment towards the existing system, disaffection, when
once stirred, spread without interruption.

It is sometimes supposed that the free-thinking and
sceptical spirit which we are accustomed to associate
with the eighteenth century, and which certainly contributed more than anything else to the colossal
destruction of '89, was also at the bottom of the overthrow of British authority in the colonies. "It was
in the insurrection of the American colonies," we
have been told, "that the great movement of the eighteenth century first assumed a violent and revolutionary
form."[1] I am unable to discover any evidence for this
in the writings or incidents of the time. The colonists
had been far out of the main current of European
thought. To this day the intellectual and spiritual
life of America shows abundantly that the philosophy
which destroyed old Europe there never sowed its
seeds. Jefferson and the lawyers introduced into the
famous document of their independence abstract doctrine borrowed from French jurists, but this, while
hurrying on the revolutionary movement in Europe,
can hardly be said to have initiated it in America.
Encyclopædists and Voltairians contributed not one

[1] Mr. Goldwin Smith on *Irish History and Irish Character*, p. 159.

solitary element to a rebellion of yeomen and traders. No reflections on the nature and obligation of the social contract paved the way for the expulsion of the instruments and apparatus of monarchy from Massachusetts and Virginia, from Pennsylvania and the Carolinas. The change was not one of those violent explosions or fundamental transformations for which in an old society it is necessary to spring a thousand different mines, or to introduce a thousand leavening conditions. There was a new and simple society, with a single tradition—resistance to oppression. The unsophisticated understandings of merchants and farmers do not require, as the members of an older society would do, to be taught how to recognise the features of oppression. Social or political injustice acquires a protective prestige by lapse of time. Men will actually pay a measure of veneration to anomalies, absurdities, iniquities, which have acquired a title to exist by prescription. Under such circumstances a prolonged and subtle inter-penetration of the national mind with ideas is the only means by which people are taught to realize the monstrousness of their case. Philosophers to fulfil this function were little needed in the American colonies. Its newness and unfamiliarity sufficed to disclose their grievance. Their origin and first history instantly reminded them of the swiftest remedy. They put it into execution with the same unyielding stubbornness with which their forefathers had resisted Elizabeth and Charles. They never faltered. When their fortunes looked least hopeful, when their dissensions among themselves were most active, they barely harboured a thought of submission. Their obstinate Hebraic creed, their recollections, their history, their rough and free manner of life, all united to shape a national character, sturdy and dauntless, not subtle or even very elevated in ideas, but with a penetrating and straight eye for such facts as came within the range of their vision, and with a resolute will which obeyed the eye.

This was the rock against which the selfishness of the English landowners, the blind obstinacy of the monarch, the incapacity of his ministers, the wrong-headed and blind pride of the ill-led masses, chose to dash. George III. and Lord North have been made scapegoats for sins which were not exclusively their own. The minister, indeed, was only the vizier, who hated his work, but still did not shrink from it, out of a sentiment that is sometimes admired under the name of loyalty, but which in such a case it is difficult to distinguish from base servility. The impenetrable

mind of the King was, in the case of the American
war, the natural organ and representative of all the
lurking ignorance and arbitrary humours of the entire
community.   It is totally unjust and inadequate to lay
upon him the entire burden.   Burke himself, in a
remarkable passage, discloses to us that for once the
king and parliament did not act without the sympathies
of the mass.   It occurs in his famous speech at Bristol,
in 1780.   He was rebuking the intolerance of those
who taunted him bitterly for the support of the
measure for the relaxation of the Penal Code against
the English Roman Catholics.   " It is but too true,"
he said, " that the love and even the very idea of
genuine liberty is extremely rare.   It is but too true
that there are many whose whole scheme of freedom
is made up of pride, perverseness, and insolence.   They
feel themselves in a state of thraldom, they imagine
that their souls are cooped and cabined in, unless they
have some man, or some body of men, dependent on
their mercy. ⌈The desire of having some one below
them descends to those who are the very lowest of all ;⌋
and a Protestant cobbler, debased by his poverty, but
exalted by his share of the ruling Church, feels a pride
in knowing it is by his generosity alone that the peer,
whose footman's instep he measures, is able to keep

his chaplain from a gaol. This disposition is the true
source of the passion which many men, in very humble
life, have taken to the American war. /*Our* subjects in
America ; *our* colonies ; *our* dependants. This lust of
party power is the liberty they hunger and thirst for ;
and this Siren song of ambition has charmed ears that
we would have thought were never organized to that
sort of music."¹/ The parallel was just. Their religious
leaders had taught the people any lesson rather than
that of an enlarged tolerance for other creeds, while
their political institutions contained no spirit and life
which, by making the whole nation participators in
their own government, might have bred a liberal
capacity of wise political judgment. Unversed in the
political art, they could have no convictions upon
political movements not directly and plainly affecting
themselves and their own condition, except such as
spring up like weeds in uncultivated ground.

Governments are the instructors, no less than the
representatives and executors, of public opinion. Public
opinion insensibly takes its colour from the governing
order and the dominant political system, wherever there
is no strong set of religious convictions, no effective
spiritual system, to engender a vigorous and indepen-

¹ Works, i. 270, *b.*

dent activity in the national mind. This was the
condition of England in the eighteenth century. The
temporary Wesleyan and Evangelical restorations of
belief had not risen to their full height in 1776. The
spiritual influence of the Established Church had fallen
pretty nearly to its lowest point. Under such circumstances, the only rulers of the mind of the nation were
its political rulers. In other words, the only general
influences which the State brought to bear upon individuals were expressly calculated to generate narrow,
rash, and arbitrary ideas. In transactions which closely
concerned their own interests, or which were believed
to concern them, the humbler classes were able to
discern the propriety and justice of popular resistance.
But where, as in the American war, they themselves
seemed to be in some sort incorporated in the imperial
authority which was disputed, popular resistance struck
them as detestable and insolent. Such a sentiment,
so far as it was to be met with in the populace, sprung
from their ignorance and short-sightedness, just as in
a loftier sphere it sprung from the ignorance and
short-sightedness of the King. The clergy, in obedience
to unfortunate though natural usage, exerted whatever
influence they may have had in favour of arbitrary
ideas, and the too frequent occasions of national fasting

were improved by angry homilies upon the wickedness of rebellion against constituted authorities.

For once in history we behold an ill-omened alliance between an arbitrary sovereign, fighting the battle of an arbitrary legislature, the aristocracy, the clergy, and the lower populace, all united to enforce oppressive claims against a distant branch of their own community. The sovereign and the humblest ranks of his subjects were actuated by the despotic ideas which are the invariable fruit of ignorance. In the critical election of 1774, for example, the popular verdict in those places where it had the best chance of being genuine was all for the ministers and the King. Westminster would have nothing to do with Burke, and returned two obscure lords of ancient lineage, the candidates of the court. The land-owning aristocracy, with their usual patriotism were thinking of saving themselves a few halfpence in the pound on the land-tax. The clergy inherited repressive tenets from many previous generations; for their Church had learnt, in Burke's gorgeous phrase, 'to exalt her mitred front in court and Parliament,' only at the expense of her freedom, her nobleness, and her spirituality. No class in the country, except the merchants, set their faces resolutely against the war. Those who did not support the measures of the court stood aside in languor and indifference. It is just possible that this was the mental attitude of a majority of the nation. It was fortunate for them and for us that the yeomen and merchants on the other side of the Atlantic had a more just and energetic appreciation of the crisis. The insurgents, while achieving their own freedom, were indirectly engaged in fighting the battle of the people of the mother country as well. / "If England prevails," said Horace Walpole, "English and American liberty is at an end." / If one fell the other would fall with it. Burke, seeing this, " certainly never could and never did wish," as he says of himself, " the colonists to be subdued by arms. He was fully persuaded that if such should be the event, they must be held in that subdued state by a great body of standing forces, and perhaps of foreign forces. He was strongly of opinion that such armies, first victorious over Englishmen, in a conflict for English constitutional rights and privileges, and afterwards habituated (though in America) to keep an English people in a state of abject subjection, would prove fatal in the end to the liberties of England itself." [2]

---

[1] *Letters,* vi. 250 (ed. 1857).
[2] *Appeal from the New to the Old Whigs,* Works, i. 504, a.

The way for this more remote peril was being sedulously prepared by a widespread deterioration among popular ideas and a fatal relaxation of the hold which they had previously gained in the public mind. " In order to prove that the Americans have no right to their liberties we are every day endeavouring to subvert the maxims which preserve the whole spirit of our own. To prove that the Americans ought not to be free we are obliged to depreciate the value of freedom itself; and we never seem to gain a paltry advantage over them in debate without attacking some of those principles or deriding some of those feelings for which our ancestors have shed their blood."[1] The material strength of the Government and its moral strength alike would have been reinforced by the defeat of the colonists to such an extent as to have seriously delayed or even jeopardised English progress, and therefore that of Europe too. As it was, public opinion was seriously demoralised by even a temporary infusion of arbitrary ideas into the popular mind.

This demoralisation may well be believed to have done something to make the task of repression easy—strangely easy, as it appears to us, fifteen years later.

[1] *Speech on Conciliation with America* (March 22, 1775), Works, i. 192, *a.*

The atrocious legislation of the last five or six years of the eighteenth century was the retribution for the lethargy or approval with which the mass of the English community had watched the measures of 1774. It is impossible to tell even how much this demoralisation of opinion of which I have spoken had to do with ⌠our pestilent and short-sighted policy in the revolutionary wars.⌡ That policy was dictated by the anger and alarm of the oligarchy. But then the oligarchy knew no better. There had been in the civil war of 1776 an opportunity of teaching them the great lesson which, sooner or later, awaits all oligarchies. But the nation was not ripe. The majority took the wrong side, and were indoctrinated with the wrong set of political maxims. Proving, as Burke said, that the colonists ought not to be free, they depreciated the value of freedom itself. The inoculation of a people with absolutist ideas is an evil process of which the results do not vanish when the external symptoms of inflammation have subsided. The political principles which gained general favour between 1770 and 1780 were the result and the expression of our social state at the time. The success of absolutism in England from 1794 was the result and the measure of the depth to which those political principles had penetrated.

The attitude of the English majority in the War of American Independence, and the wretched disasters which ensued, constitute one of the most striking examples which history furnishes of the wide-spread mischief that may be inflicted by the predominance of an unsound metaphysical abstraction. The abstract conception which wrought such evil at this lamentable period is still full of noxious vitality—an unfortunate fact which makes the study of these events particularly pregnant with instruction to those who have not been led to abandon the notion upon other grounds. It may perhaps be a question with the student of history, whether the misdirected idea of public Right, or the misdirected idea of public Duty, has been the root of greater calamities for mankind. To the latter we owe the chapter of religious persecution, which might appear the most heartrending section in the annals of the race, until we come to reflect on the misery which has been spread over the face of the earth in the vindication of their fancied or real rights by tyrannical sovereigns and frenzied peoples. The motive present to the earliest English supporters of Lord North's system was mainly a desire to save themselves from a part of their taxes, which they hoped to extract from the colonists. But a mercenary impulse of this sort must be supported and justified by a passable principle. Without such a principle they would not be able to grapple to themselves the mass of the people. They fell back upon the doctrine that the English Government was sovereign in the colonies as at home ; and in the notion of sovereignty they found inherent the notion of an indefeasible right to impose and exact taxes. Having satisfied themselves of the existence of this sovereignty and of the right, therefore, which they took to be its natural property, they saw no step between the establishment of their abstract right and the establishment of the propriety of en- forcing it. To enforce a right seemed to them as indisputably natural and proper as it is to believe a truth which has once been made to present itself to the mind. We have no alternative but to admit a truth as soon as we are persuaded that it is one. We have no alternative but to claim and execute a right which we have once proved to exist. Nothing beyond this item of proof seemed to be required to warrant the advance to active measures.

For an illustration of the vitality which still exists in this mode of thinking in politics, we need go no further than the tone too generally adopted in England during the slavery contest in the United States. People convinced themselves, some after careful examination of the documents on which the constitutional questions turned, others by mere cursory glances at second-hand authorities, that the Southern States had a *right* to secede. Satisfied so far, they needed no more than this to assure them that their sympathies might lawfully flow to the side in which they had discovered a documentary and constitutional right. The current of feeling was precisely similar in the struggle to which the United States owed their separate existence. Right was raised to be an omnipotent and infallible divinity, into whose nature and foundation no further inquiry was permissible. It was an ultimate fact, an idea incapable of resolution into simpler elements. Other figments of metaphysicians have been elevated to the same mysterious level, overriding the demands of progress, drowning the voice of practical sense, and consigning one generation of men after another to live for much of their lives in fools' paradises. None of these figments is more monstrous than this of the final and absolute existence of a Right. As if Right in the highest sense of all were something beyond analysis and beyond a test, and, still more absurd and mischievous, as if any given right were possessed of qualities beyond those of a measurable, fluctuating,

and conventional value, assigned to it by its greater
or less conformity with the conditions of the general
convenience.   As soon as a right, that of taxing a
colony or any other, ceases to harmonize with prudence and expediency, to insist upon it is deliberately
to clasp disaster to your arms.   This was exactly what
the English nation did in considering its own position
towards the colonists.

The question to be asked by every statesman and
every citizen with reference to a measure that is
recommended to him as the enforcement of a public
right, is whether the right is one which it is to the
public advantage to enforce.   Burke's mind, thoroughly
penetrated with these considerations, was led by them
at once to grasp the true principle of conduct throughout the course of the transactions between England
and the colonies.   The idea of a right as a mysterious
and reverend abstraction, to be worshipped in a state
of naked divorce from expediency and convenience,
was one that his political judgment found preposterous
and unendurable.   He hated the arbitrary and despotic
savour which clung about the English assumptions
over the colonies.   And his repulsion was heightened
when he found that these assumptions were justified,
not by some permanent advantage which their victory

would procure for the mother country or for the colonies, or which would repay the cost of gaining such a victory, not by the assertion and demonstration of some positive duty, but by the futile and meaningless doctrine that we had a right to do something or other, if we liked. That this should be looked upon as a conclusive argument, when in truth it was all but irrelevant, excited all that passion which Burke's intense thoroughness kept ever ready to burst forth into flame.

The folly of clamouring in vindication of rights which were burdened with conditions that made them much worse than valueless, stirred him beyond patience. The alleged compromise of the national dignity implied in a withdrawal of the just claim of the Government, instead of convincing, only exasperated him. Dignity, he bade them remember, had of late been a sheer incumbrance, at war with their interest and with every idea of their policy. " Show the thing you contend for to be reason ; show it to be common sense ; show it to be the means of attaining some useful end ; and then I am content to allow it what dignity you please." [1] The year after this, he took up the same ground still more firmly, and explained it still more

[1] *Speech on American Taxation,* Works, i. 158, *b.*

L 2

impressively. As for the question of the right of taxation, he exclaimed, " It is less than nothing in my consideration. . . . . My consideration is narrow, confined, and wholly limited to the policy of the question. I do not examine whether the giving away a man's money be a power excepted and reserved out of the general trust of Government; and how far all forms of polity are entitled to an exercise of that right by the charter of nature. Or whether, on the contrary, a right of taxation is necessarily involved in the general principle of legislation, and inseparable from the ordinary supreme power. These are deep questions where great names militate against each other ; where reason is perplexed ; and an appeal to authorities only thickens the confusion. For high and reverend authorities lift up their heads on both sides, and there is no sure footing in the middle. This point is ' the great Serbonian bog, betwixt Damiata and Mount Casius old, where armies whole have sunk.' I do not intend to be overwhelmed in that bog, though in such respectable company. *The question with me is not whether you have a right to render your people miserable, but whether it is not your interest to make them happy.* It is not what a lawyer tells me I *may* do, but what humanity, reason, and justice tell me I *ought* to do. Is a politic act the worse for being a generous one ? Is no concession proper but that which is made from your want of right to keep what you grant ? Or does it lessen the grace and dignity of relaxing in the exercise of an odious claim, because you have your evidence-room full of titles, and your magazines stuffed with arms to enforce them ?

"What signify all these titles and all these arms ? Of what avail are they, when the reason of the thing tells me that the assertion of my title is the loss of my suit; and that I could do nothing but wound myself by the use of my own weapons ? Such is steadfastly my opinion of the absolute necessity of keeping up the concord of this empire by a unity of spirit, though in a diversity of operations, that if I were sure the colonists had, at their leaving this country, sealed a regular compact of servitude; that they solemnly abjured all the rights of citizens; that they had made a vow to renounce all ideas of liberty for them and their posterity to all generations, yet I should hold myself obliged to conform to the temper I found universally prevalent in my own day, and to govern two millions of men impatient of servitude, on the principles of freedom. I am not determining a point of law; I am restoring tranquillity, and the general character and situation of a people must determine what sort of government is fitted for them."[1]

The defenders of expediency as the criterion of morals are commonly charged by their opponents with holding a doctrine that lowers the moral capabilities, and that would ruin society if it were unfortunately to gain general acceptance. The king and the minister in 1774 entertained this view, and scorned to submit their policy to so mean a test as that prescribed by the creed of utility. If they had listened to the voice of the most eloquent and sagacious of the upholders of this test, they would have saved the empire. If they had for a moment awakened to the utilitarian truth, that the statesman is concerned, not at all with the rights of the government, but altogether with the interests and happiness of the governed; if they had weighed their policy in the capacious balance of expediency, rather than with the airy, unreal, deceptive apparatus of the abstract principles of sovereignty, at least the separation of the mother country from her too powerful sons might have been effected as such a change ought to have been effected. As it was, the disaster in which they were finally overwhelmed formed an expressive comment upon the supremacy of

[1] *Speech on Conciliation with America*, Works, i. 192, *a*.

the metaphysical notion of absolute right in practical politics. The actual bearings of circumstances, so visible to anybody who, like Burke, looked upon them from the point of high practical sense, were hidden from the sight of men who surrounded themselves with a hazy medium of abstract and universally applicable ideas. The conception of an indefeasible right of sovereignty blinded them. It was they who were thus kept grovelling along the lowest ground, while their opponents, who chose to measure their policy by the standard of convenience, of the interest of the greatest number, of utility and expediency, were guided by it to the loftiest heights of political wisdom and beneficence.

The baneful superstition that there is in morals, and in the art of politics, therefore, which is a province of morals, some supernaturally illumined lamp, still survives to make men neglect the intelligible and available tests of public convenience and practical justice, which is no more than expediency in its widest shape. If Burke were among us at this day, enjoining habitual recourse in every political measure to this standard, he would find that men are nearly as disposed as ever to reason downwards from high-sounding ideas of Right, Sovereignty, Property, and so forth; which have in

truth no invariable conformity to facts, and which are
only treated with reverence because they are absurdly
supposed to be ultimate, eternal entities, incapable of
further resolution.   Are we sure that if a set of conditions similar to those of 1776 were to recur in our own
time, we should be wise enough to toss aside lawyers'
questions as to the exact measure and boundaries of
our rights, and examine positively and simply what
would be the course most likely to reconcile the best
interests of all the people concerned ?   If anybody is
sure of this, let him look at Ireland and the policy
of the landowners' party in that country.

The same vicious spirit of adherence to the very
letter of legal or quasi-constitutional rights had ever
marked the whole policy of England towards her
American dependencies.   It was the same spirit which,
long before Grenville's scheme of taxation, had planted
and nourished the germs of discord between the mother
country and the colonies.   The Stamp Act and the
Tea Duty were no more than the last drops in a full
cup.   They were the assertion of a right of one kind,
made without any thought as to the profit to be
drawn from it.   The laws regulating the commerce of
the colonies were the assertion of a right of another

kind, left equally unexamined by the only test proper to it. The policy pursued in the former instance by the Ministry and the landowning aristocracy and the people over whom these had influence, and in the latter instance by the merchants, was in either case the creature of an arbitrary persuasion of a right in the mother country to do whatever she might deem convenient to her own interests with her colonies, without thought or heed for their welfare. The merchants detested and opposed the war with all their might. But it was they who had sown the seed. Their folly was eclipsed by the infatuation of the Government, but if the landowners fancied that the colonists existed for the purpose of saving them the land-tax, at least they could allege in their excuse the creed of the merchants, that colonies existed for the purpose of enlarging the profits of the home traders.

Historians, in treating of the American rebellion, have confined their arguments too exclusively to the question of internal taxation, and the right or policy of exercising this prerogative. The true source of the rebellion lay deeper, in our traditional colonial policy. Just as the Spaniards had been excited to the discovery of America by the hope of obtaining gold and silver, the

English merchants utilized the discovery by the same fallacious method, and with the same fallacious aspirations. Each wished to bring as much as they could of the precious metals to Europe, and each, with true commercial selfishness, disregarded the interests of the inhabitants whom they found there. Each brought down retribution upon their country, though in unequal measure. Spain was undone by the influx of gold, and by the diversion of her industry from manufactures to the gold mines. England had to endure first the material loss produced by the short-sighted rapacity of her traders, and then both the ignominy and the material loss combined, which flowed from the rapacity of her aristocracy and the incompetency of her patrician administrators. The Mercantile System is now so stone-dead, that we forget that only a hundred years ago it was full of animation, the key to our whole commercial policy, the great check to industrial growth, the pertinacious and obstructive relic of mediæval superstitions about the mysterious virtues of gold. A hundred years ago the commercial classes believed that the prime object of their pursuits was to get as much gold and silver into England as they could. They sought, therefore, to make their country, as nearly as they might, a solitary centre of the exportation of non-metallic commodities, that so she might be also the great reservoir into which the precious metals would flow in a return stream. On this base their colonial policy was erected. Here, it may be noted in passing, was the secret of English foreign policy from shortly before the fall of Walpole—extension of markets, with England as the centre whence commodities might be diffused. This was the national idea throughout the middle portion of the eighteenth century, the century of commercial wars. The colonies had their place allotted, to them in the system. They were to help to swell the stream. Some of the most important of their productions were confined to the English market, and could be exported to no other country. In the same spirit, they were prohibited from importing from any other country. Provinces, even, were forbidden to import certain commodities from their neighbouring provinces. Everything which Europe most needed from the colonies was to come through English markets. Everything which the colonies most needed from Europe, and some things which they needed from each other, were equally to come through English markets. It has been urged that, while we dwell on the commercial restrictions under which the colonists laboured, we forget the commercial privileges which they enjoyed. "If the English were to be debarred from smoking any but Virginian-grown tobacco," Lord Stanhope says, "there seems the less hardship in debarring the Virginians from wearing any but English-made cloth."[1] The one, he thinks, ought fairly to be reckoned as some counterpoise to the other. But the value of the privilege was trifling in comparison with the detriment done by the restriction. The protection of one or two of their products was a small gain to set against the double evil, of their partial exclusion from the great European markets, first as sellers, and second as buyers. To inflict a slight loss on ourselves was not to make up for the infliction of a gigantic loss upon the colonists. This is not to introduce a counterpoise, but only to complete a circle of wrong.

So long as the colonies remained in their infancy the mercantile policy was less prejudicial to their interests. The monopoly of their commerce, the limitation of their markets, the discouragement of their manufactures, in some cases amounting to absolute prohibition, were all less fatal in a country where labour was dear, than they would be in a state where population was more fully developed and land

---

[1] *History of England*, v. 81.

had become scarcer. Still, the best that Adam Smith could find to say of the policy of England towards her colonies was that it was somewhat less illiberal and oppressive than that pursued by other mother-countries. [1]

The opposition, however, between this artificial system and visible needs and circumstances was too fundamental to be shirked. The urgency of facts made a way of escape. "C'est à la contrebande," Blanqui says generally, "que le commerce doit de n'avoir pas péri sous l'influence du régime prohibitif, tandis que ce régime condamnait les peuples à s'approvisionner aux sources les plus éloignées, la contrebande rapprochait les distances, abaissait les prix, et neutralisait l'influence funeste des monopoles." [2] It was so with the American colonies. A contraband trade sprung up between them and the colonies of Spain. Our settlers imported goods from England, and re-exported them to the Spanish colonies, in return for

---

[1] *Wealth of Nations*, book iv. ch. vii. pt. 2. There is in the same place (p. 262, of McCulloch's edition, 1855) an illustration of the way in which the merchants, the principal advisers of the various regulations of trade, sacrificed the interests not only of the colonies, but of the mother country into the bargain, even as those interests were then understood.

[2] *Histoire de l'Économie Politique*, ii. 25.

bullion and other commodities. The result of this was that the Spanish colonists had access to useful commodities from which they would otherwise have been debarred, that the American colonists could without distress remit the specie which was required by the nature of their dealings with England, and that a large market was opened for English products. This widely beneficial trade was incontinently suppressed in 1764, by one of those efforts of short-sighted rigour which might be expected from any government where George Grenville's influence was prominent. All smuggling was to be put down, and as this trade was contraband, it must be put down like the rest. The Government probably acted as they did in answer to the prayers of the mercantile classes, who could not see that they were cutting off the streams that fed their own prosperity. They only saw that a colonial trade had sprung up, and their jealousy blinded them to the benefits that accrued to themselves as a consequence of it. Their folly found them out. The suppression of the colonial trade was entrusted to the commanders. of men-of-war. We have had some experience within very recent times of the arbitrary violence, the crass ignorance of law and legal usage, the barbarous insolence, which too often mark people of this kind when they are temporarily invested with civil authority. We may be sure that they were a great deal more unfit to exercise such authority a hundred years ago than they are even now. We may be sure that the original grievance of the colonists was not softened by the manners of the officers who had to put the law into execution.

The result of the whole transaction was the birth of a very strong sense in the minds of the colonists that the mother country looked upon them as a sponge to be squeezed. This conviction took more than a passing hold upon them. It was speedily inflamed into inextinguishable heat, first by the news that they were to be taxed without their own consent, and next by the tyrannical and atrocious measures by which it was proposed to crush their resistance.[1] The rebellion may be characterised as having first originated in the blind greediness of the English merchants, and as having then been precipitated by the arbitrary ideas of the patricians, in the first instance, and afterwards of the King and

---

[1] Notably by the Duke of Bedford's suggestion that a statute of the reign of Henry VIII. for trying in England persons accused of treason without the realm, should be applied to the Boston leaders. Burke's forcible denunciation of this truly execrable project may be found in the letter to the Sheriffs of Bristol. (Works, i. 206.)

the least educated of the common people. If the severe pressure of the mercantile policy, unflinchingly carried out, had not first filled the colonists with resentment and robbed them of their prosperity, the imperial claim to impose taxes would probably have been submitted to without much ado. And if the suppression of their trade in 1764 had not been instantly followed by Grenville's plan for extorting revenue from them, they would probably in time have been reconciled to the blow which had been dealt to their commerce. It was the conjunction of two highly oppressive pieces of policy which taught them that they would certainly lose more by tame compliance than they could possibly lose by an active resistance.

The conflict was thus a shock in which substantial circumstance encountered a pair of phantoms, the Mercantile Policy and the devotion to barren Rights. False ideas often gain temporary victories over the facts which they no longer cover. In this instance the superior material force and energy happened to be on the side of the facts from the first. The intellectual error of the mercantile system, and the moral error of regarding every fancied or real right as a possession to be vindicated at all hazard and all cost, were thrust into the lower place proper to them. The claim of actual circumstance to have ideas adjusted to its visible requirements, was triumphantly made good, with a rapidity and completeness of which, alas! history furnishes too few examples.

Much ridicule, a little of it not altogether undeserved, has been thrown upon the opening clause of the Declaration of Independence, which asserts the inherent natural right of man to enjoy life and liberty, with the means of acquiring and possessing property, and pursuing and obtaining happiness and safety. Yet there is an implied corollary in this which enjoins the highest morality that in our present state we are able to think of as possible. If happiness is the right of our neighbour, then not to hinder him, but to help him in its pursuit, must plainly be our duty. If all men have a claim, then each man is under an obligation. The corollary thus involved is the corner-stone of morality. It was an act of good augury thus to inscribe happiness as entering at once into the right of all, and into the duty of all, in the very head and front of the new charter, as the base of a national existence, and the first principle of a national government. The omen has not been falsified. The Americans have been true to their first doctrine. They have never swerved aside to set up caste and privilege, to lay down

the doctrine that one man's happiness ought to be an
object of greater solicitude to society than any other
man's, or that one order should be encouraged to seek
its prosperity through the depression of any other order.
Their example proved infectious. ⌠The assertion in the
New World, that men have a right to happiness and
an obligation to promote the happiness of one another,
struck a spark in the Old World. Political construction
in America immediately preceded the last violent stage
of demolition in Europe.

Burke must often have thought deeply of the destinies of the kindred nation with whose independence
his own efforts will ever be so indissolubly associated.
But all his reflections upon the future of America,
notwithstanding his conviction that her independence
was the necessary price of the maintenance of free
government in England, must have been tinged with
bitterness. Great as America might become, and as
he honestly wished her to become, her greatness would
bring no renown or laud to the mother-country, or its
incomparable Constitution. Though above the narrow
vices incident to patriotism in weaker and less loftily
moral souls, it could not have been more grievous to
him to look back upon the circumstances under which
England and her sons parted company, than it was

mortifying to look forward to a glory for America which, if statesmen had been prescient and nations just, might have been added to the abundant glories of England. Burke, we may be sure, had none of that speculative fortitude which enabled Adam Smith to anticipate with composure the possible removal of the seat of empire to that part of the empire which in a century (from 1776) would probably contribute most to the general defence.[1] He was intellectually capable of foreseeing much which he was not morally capable of allowing himself fully to realise, and certainly not of constraining himself to dwell upon.

To the student of human history who lives in later times, there are few objects of meditation so interesting as the probable course of evolution in the great empire whose origin we have been considering. The conditions are in some respects so profoundly different from those which have to be taken into account in observing the development of European civilization, while at the same time there has been such a constant and reciprocal action at work between America and Europe, that our usual historic apparatus misses its hold and application. It is comparatively simple to trace the elements which America contributes to the decomposition of the old,

[1] *Wealth of Nations*, bk. iv. c. vii. pt. 3, p. 282 (ed. of 1855).

and the construction of the new state in Europe. But how, with our ordinary methods, can we discern the main currents of the history of a country, first incongruously colonized by Swedes, Dutch, French, Spanish, and English; which has never undergone the harmonizing and binding influence of an uniform spiritual belief; which daily receives enormous bodies of immigrants with as many ways of thinking as there are bodies, about religion and government, about the past and the future; whose territorial consolidation is not yet accomplished,—how can we analyse, or understand, or characterise, a national organization that exists under such conditions as these? how attempt as yet to assign a place in the history of mankind to the event which propelled America far out of the grooves along which we continue our course, into new and unfamiliar channels of its own? /For the philosophy of American history, the exposition of its moral forces, its root-ideas, its expanding elements,—for this we shall have long to wait. 7

CHAPTER V.

ECONOMICAL REFORM, IRELAND, AND INDIA.

THE statesman who resists all projects for the reform of the constitution, and yet eagerly proclaims how deplorably imperfect are the practical results of its working, binds himself to vigorous exertions for the amendment of administration. Burke devoted himself to this duty with a fervid assiduity that has not often been exampled, and has never been surpassed. Just as an Irish clansman would have anxiously explained the crimes of his chieftain by evil counsellors and unhappy circumstance, so Burke insisted on explaining the disorders which abounded on every side of him by the wickedness or folly of individuals, rather than he would allow any slur to rest on the constitution for which he had so devoted an affection. This made him indefatigable in his enmity to everything that savoured of abuse and mal-administration. He went to work with the zeal of a religious enthusiast, intent on purging his church and his faith of the corruptions which lowered it in the eyes of men. There was no part or order of government so obscure, so remote, or so complex, as to escape his acute and persevering observation.

Apart from his intense faith in the constitution, Burke had, what is the emphatically distinctive mark of the great statesman—the Richelieu, the Cromwell, the Charles III.—a passion for good, wise, and orderly government. For all that wore the look of confusion, he had an abhorrence that made other men marvel, and he detected the elements and seed of confusion with a perspicacity that made other men despair. This temper was not the product of any innate and reckless sympathy with the firm and energetic exercise of power for power's own sake. /The modern barbarous, immoral, and retrograde cant of hero-worship would have filled him with repugnance. Warren Hastings was thought the most successful administrative genius of his time, but he was violent and unscrupulous. Burke pursued him with merciless indignation, and covered him with embarrassment and ruin. He detested folly and cruelty in high places, everything that was either imbecile or arbitrary, because his vivid imagination and excessive sensibility revealed to him in their fullest size and most striking colours the sufferings which were thus entailed on those who dwelt in lower place. His keen feeling for good government was the fruit of his zeal for the happiness and well-being of every creature within the sphere of government. In the three fields of his activity over which we shall now but too quickly proceed, nothing is so conspicuous and impressive as this loftily social point of view. The most wearisome details of questions, now this long while settled and forgotten, receive a suffusion of interest and colour from the constant play around them of wide and rich human wisdom. Whatever he handled,—the flagitious expenditure of the public resources, the wrongs of the Irish merchant or the Irish Catholic peasant, the rapacity of English adventurers in India, the crimes of the imperial Hastings,—all was treated with that nobility of idea and expression which mere talent is invariably the better for studying, but which is only inborn, familiar, and perfect, in a few men of fine genius and deep morality of nature. Passion left flaws to offend a fastidious taste, and too frequently marked his gravity with exaggeration and his humour with clumsiness. But these were mainly accidents of atmosphere. Notwithstanding them, we look in vain elsewhere in the history of English politics for the illumination of such questions as those before us, by such amplitude of knowledge, united to so much comprehension, force, and elevation.

I. Burke's object, in his schemes for Economical Reform, was less to husband the public resources and relieve the tax-payer—though this aim could not have been absent from his mind, overburdened as England then was with the charges of the American War—than to cut off the channels which supplied the corruption of the House of Commons. The full title of the first project which he presented to the legislature (February, 1780), was "A Plan for the Better Security of the Independence of Parliament, and the Economical Reformation of the Civil and other Establishments." It was to the former that he deemed the latter to be the most direct road. The strength of the administration in the House was due to the gifts which the Minister had in his hands to dispense. Men voted with the side which could reward their fidelity. It was the number of sinecure places and unpublished pensions, which along with the controllable influence of peers and nabobs, furnished the Minister with an irresistible lever: the avarice and the degraded public spirit of the recipients supplied the required fulcrum. Burke knew that in sweeping away these factitious places and secret pensions he would be robbing the Court of its chief implements of corruption, and protecting the representative against his chief motive in selling his country. He conceived that he would thus be promoting a far more infallible means than any scheme of electoral reform could have provided, for reviving the integrity and independence of the House of Commons. In his eyes, the evil resided not in the constituencies, but in their representatives ; not in the small number of the one, but in the smaller integrity of the other.

The evil did not stop where it began. It was not merely that the sinister motive thus engendered in the minds of too lax and facile men induced them to betray their legislative trust, and barter their own uprightness and the interests of the State. The acquisition of one of these nefarious bribes meant much more than a sinister vote. It called into existence a champion of every inveterate abuse that weighed on the resources of the country. There is a well-known passage in the speech on Economical Reform, in which the speaker shows what an insurmountable obstacle Lord Talbot had found in his attempt to carry out certain reforms in the royal household, in the fact that the turnspit of the King's kitchen was a member of Parliament. " On that rock his whole adventure split,—his whole scheme of economy was dashed to pieces; his department became more expensive than ever; the Civil List debt accumulated." Interference with the expenses of the household meant interference with the perquisites or fees of this legislative turnspit, and the rights of sinecures were too sacred to be touched. In comparison with them, it counted for nothing that the King's tradesmen went unpaid, and became bankrupt; that the judges were unpaid; that "the justice of the kingdom bent and gave way; the foreign ministers remained inactive and unprovided; the system of Europe was dissolved; the chain of our alliances was broken; all the wheels of Government at home and abroad were stopped. *The king's turnspit was a member of Parliament.*" [1] This office and numbers of others exactly like it, existed solely because the House of Commons was crowded with venal men. The post of royal scullion meant a vote that could be relied upon under every circumstance and in all emergencies. And each incumbent of such an office felt his honour and interests concerned in the defence of all other offices of the

---

[1] *Economical Reform*, Works, i. 240, *a*. The Civil List at this time comprehended a great number of charges, such as those of which Burke speaks, that had nothing to do with the sovereign personally. They were slowly removed, the judicial and diplomatic charges being transferred, on the accession of William IV.

same scandalous description. There was thus maintained a strong standing army of expensive, lax, and corrupting officials.

The royal household was a gigantic nest of costly jobbery and purposeless profusion. It retained all "the cumbrous charge of a Gothic establishment," though all its usage and accommodation had "shrunk into the polished littleness of modern elegance." The outlay was enormous. The expenditure on the court tables only, was a thing unfathomable. Waste was the rule in every branch of it. There was an office for the Great Wardrobe, another office of the Robes, a third of the Groom of the Stole. For these three useless offices there were three useless treasurers. They all laid a heavy burden on the taxpayer, in order to supply a bribe to the member of parliament. The plain remedy was to annihilate the subordinate treasuries. "Take away," was Burke's demand, "the whole establishment of detail in the household : the Treasurer, the Comptroller, the Cofferer of the Household, the Treasurer of the Chamber, the Master of the Household, the whole Board of Green Cloth ; a vast number of subordinate offices in the department of the Steward of the Household ; the whole establishment of the Great Wardrobe ; the Removing Wardrobe ; the Jewel Office ; the Robes ;

the Board of Works." The abolition of this monstrously cumbrous system would not only diminish expense, and promote efficiency ; it would do still more excellent service in destroying the roots of parliamentary corruption. " Under other governments a question of expense is only a question of economy; and it is nothing more ; with us, in every question of expense, there is always a mixture of constitutional considerations." [1]

Places and pensions, though the worst, were not by any means the only stumbling-block in the way of pure and well-ordered government. The administration of the estates of the Crown,—the Principality, the Duchy of Cornwall, the Duchy of Lancaster, the County Palatine of Chester,—was an elaborate system of confused and unprofitable expenditure. Wales had to herself eight judges, while no more than twelve sufficed to perform the whole business of justice in England, a country ten times as large, and a hundred times as opulent. Wales, and each of the duchies, had its own exchequer. Every one of these principalities, said Burke, has the apparatus of a kingdom for the jurisdiction over a few private estates ; and the formality and charge of the Exchequer of Great Britain for

[1] *Economical Reform*, Works, i. 242.

collecting the rents of a country squire. They were the field, in his expressive phrase, of mock jurisdictions and mimic revenues, of difficult trifles and laborious fooleries. " It was but the other day that that pert factious fellow, the Duke of Lancaster, presumed to fly in the face of his liege lord, our gracious sovereign—presumed to go to law with the King. The object is neither your business nor mine. Which of the parties got the better I really forget. The material point is that the suit cost about 15,000*l*. But as the Duke of Lancaster is but agent of Duke Humphrey and not worth a groat, our sovereign was obliged to pay the costs of both."[1] The system which involved these costly absurdities, Burke proposed entirely to abolish. In the same spirit he wished to dispose of the Crown lands and the forest lands, which it was for the good of the community, not less than of the Crown itself, to throw into the hands of private owners.

One of the most important of these projected reforms and one which its author did not flinch from carrying out two years later, to his own loss, related to the office of Paymaster. This functionary was accustomed to hold large balances of the public money in his own hands, and for his own profit, for long periods, owing

[1] *Economical Reform*, Works, i. 236, *a*.

to a complex system of accounts, which was so rigorous as entirely to defeat its own object.[1] The Paymaster could not, through the multiplicity of forms and the exaction of impossible conditions, get a prompt acquittance. The audit sometimes did not take place for years after the accounts were virtually closed. Meanwhile, the money accumulated in his hands, and its profits were his legitimate perquisite. The first Lord Holland, for example, held the balances of his office from 1765, when he retired, until 1778, when they were audited. During this time he realized, as the interest on the use of these balances, nearly two hundred and fifty thousand pounds. Burke diverted these enormous gains into the coffers of the state. He fixed the Paymaster's salary at four thousand pounds a year, and was himself the first person who accepted the curtailed income.

The economical reforms which were actually effected when the Whigs came into power on the fall of Lord North, fell short by a long way of those which Burke had so industriously devised and so forcibly recommended. Patrician Whigs in power have seldom shown themselves inferior in rapacity to their rivals. In 1782, while Burke declined to spare his own office,

---

[1] *Economical Reform*, Works, i. 242-3.

the chief of the cabinet which Burke was not high-born enough to enter, conferred upon Barré a pension of over three thousand a year; above ten times the amount, as has been said, which, in Lord Rockingham's own judgment, as expressed in the new Bill, ought henceforth to be granted to any one person whatever.[1] This shortcoming, however, does not detract from Burke's distinguished merit. The eloquence, industry, ingenuity, above all, the sagacity and the justice of this great effort of 1780, are none the less worthy of our admiration and regard because, in 1782, his patrician chiefs, partly in accordance with their own predatory traditions, partly perhaps out of a revived deference for the feelings of their royal master, showed that the possession of office had sensibly cooled the ardent aspirations proper to Opposition.

Not the most fervid or brilliant of Burke's pieces yet the speech on economical reform is certainly not the least instructive or impressive of them. It gives us a suggestive view of the relations existing at that time between the House of Commons and the Court. It discloses to us the sordid and unpatriotic spirit of the monarch and the ministers who could resist proposals so reasonable in themselves, and so alleviating

[1] Earl Stanhope's *History of England.* vii. 165.

in their effects, at a time when the nation was suffering
the heavy and distressing burdens of the most disastrous
war that this country has ever carried on.   It is especially interesting as the most perfect illustration of
its author's political capacity.   At a moment when
committees, and petitions, and great county meetings
showed how thoroughly the national anger was roused
against the existing system, Burke came to the front
of affairs with a scheme, the most striking characteristic of which proved to be that it was so profoundly
temperate.   Bent on the extirpation of the system, he
had no demagogic ill-will towards the men who had
happened to grow up and to flourish in it.   " I never
will suffer," he said, " any man or description of men
to suffer from errors that naturally have grown out
of the abusive constitution of those offices which I
propose to regulate.   If I cannot reform with equity,
I will not reform at all."   Exasperated as he was by
the fruitlessness of his opposition to a policy which
he detested from the bottom of his soul, it would
have been little wonderful if he had resorted to every
weapon of his unrivalled rhetorical armoury, in order
to discredit and overthrow the entire scheme of
government.   Yet nothing could have been further
from his mind than any violent or extreme idea of

this sort. Many years afterwards he took credit to himself less for what he did on this occasion, than on what he prevented from being done. People were ready for a new modelling of the two Houses of Parliament, as well as for grave modifications of the Prerogative. Burke resisted this temper unflinchingly. "I had," he says, "a state to preserve, as well as a state to reform, I had a people to gratify, but not to inflame or to mislead." He then recounts without exaggeration the pains and caution with which he sought reform, while steering clear of innovation. "I heaved the lead every inch of way, I made."[1] It is grievous to think that a man who could assume such an attitude at such a time, who could give such proof of his profound skill in the great, the difficult, art of governing, was allowed to do no more than hold a fifth-rate office for some time less than a twelvemonth.

II. Unlike too many Irishmen, Burke was never so absorbed in other public affairs as to forget the peculiar interests of his native country. We have his own word, which his career does not belie, that in the elation with which he was filled on being elected a member of Parliament, what was first and uppermost

[1] *Letter to a Noble Lord*, Works, ii. 262.

in his thoughts was the hope of being somewhat useful to the place of his birth and education.[1] So much mischief has been done by the superficial and incidental kind of treatment which Irish history has usually received, that I would gladly have avoided a subject which here I can scarcely treat other than superficially and incidentally. To understand a simple epoch, however narrow, or a single public event, however seemingly isolated, it is necessary to have an exceptionally comprehensive grasp of the whole chain and sequence of Irish progress. It is for lack of this that that progress has been so tardy. The geographical proximity of Ireland has misled politicians into the habit of explaining all that happens there by the usual reference to the general ideas, passions, and common movements, of the rest of civilized Europe. The truth is, that Irish evolution has moved in an independent course. To assume its identity with the general Western development is as extravagant as such an assumption would be in the case of Jamaica or the Cape of Good Hope.

Surveying Europe for the last five centuries, we

---

[1] *Letter to Thomas Burgh, Esq.*, Works, ii. 413, *b.* The fragment upon the Irish Popery Laws is believed to have been composed about 1765, the time of his entry into public life.

see feudalism and Catholicism decaying, principles of
toleration expanding into wider and wider acceptance,
the gradual substitution of positive and scientific
habits of thought for the barren methods of theological or metaphysical superstition, the rapid advance
of industry, and the growth in importance and consideration of the industrial classes. Turning from
this to Ireland, we meet a widely different picture.
These various transformations have never been undergone by her. Instead of Catholicism decaying, we
see it rooted and fostered by its identification with
hostility to the political oppressor. Instead of a crum-
bling feudalism, we encounter all the worst attributes
of an era of conquest, aggravated by the circumstance
of its extreme untimeousness. Instead of the growth
of toleration, we find at the very end of the tolerant
eighteenth century, Catholic and Protestant engaged
in a violent and sanguinary struggle. Instead of the
slow replacement of superstition by reason, we see
Ireland the chief home of the most irrational forms
of Ultramontanism, we see religious considerations
paramount in determining political attitudes, and we
see Irish Liberals deliberately abandoning the only
principles on which their country could be freed from
its oppressive system, because those principles would

deprive the Pope of his temporalities. In spite of
the root and branch policy of the Tudors, of the great
re-organization of James I., of the Cromwellian paci-
fication, of the Restoration settlement, and the Revolution settlement, in spite of all that has been done in
the last century and in this, the primitive conception
of property remains strong and vivid in the mind of
the Irish peasant, and to understand the agrarianism
of to-day we have to go far back to the barbarous
period, when the land was not the property of the
chief or the individual, but belonged in common
ownership to the whole Sept. The ancient organization was never dissolved. New forms were imposed
by the English conquerors, but the old ideas remained
in active vitality underneath.[1]

Ireland in the middle of the eighteenth century was
to England just what the American colonies would
have been, if they had contained, besides the European
settlers, more than twice their number of unenslaved

---

[1] It has been judiciously observed, that the stage which Irish revolution had reached when these various settlements of the land were
made was the secret of Irish disaffection being so broad and deep. If
he land had belonged to a body of nobles, its confiscation would only
have aggrieved a small caste. As it was, every member of a sept
looked upon himself as a landowner. (Cf. M'Lennan's *Memoir of Thomas
Drummond*, p. 219.)

negroes. After the suppression of the great rebellion of Tyrconnel by William of Orange, nearly the whole of the land was confiscated, the peasants were made beggars and outlaws, the Penal Laws against the Catholics were enacted and enforced, and the grand reign of Protestant Ascendancy began in all its vileness and completeness. The Protestants and landlords were supreme ; the peasants and the Catholics were prostrate in despair. The Revolution brought about in Ireland just the reverse of what it effected in England. Here it delivered the body of the nation from the attempted supremacy of a small sect. There it made a small sect supreme over the body of the nation. " It was, to say the truth," Burke wrote, " not a revolution but a conquest," and the policy of conquest was treated as the just and normal system of government, proper for all time. Our last conquest was in the eleventh century. The last conquest of Ireland was at the very end of the seventeenth.

Sixty years later some important changes had taken place. The English settlers of the beginning of the century had formed an Irish interest. They had become Anglo-Irish, just as the colonists still further west had formed a colonial interest and become Anglo-American. The same conduct on the part of the mother country promoted the growth of these hostile interests in both cases. We have seen in the preceding chapter the commercial policy pursued by England towards America. Here we need only remember that it was identical with that pursued towards Ireland. The industry of the Anglo-Irish traders was restricted, their commerce and even their production fettered, their prosperity checked, for the benefit of the merchants of Manchester and Bristol. / *Crescit Roma Albæ ruinis.* / On the other hand, the peasantry had gradually taken heart to resent their spoliation and attempted extirpation, and in 1761 their misery under the exactions of landlords and a Church which tried to spread Christianity by the brotherly agency of the tithe-proctor, gave birth to Whiteboyism — a terrible spectre, which, under various names and with various modifications, has ridden Ireland down to this time.

In 1765, then, when Burke came into Parliament, he saw the Protestant traders of the dependency the victims of the colonial and commercial system ; the Catholic landowners dispossessed by the operation of the penal laws ; the Catholic peasantry—being twice as numerous as their masters—deeply penetrated with an insurgent and vindictive spirit ; and the imperial government standing very much aloof, and leaving the country to the tender mercies of the Undertakers and some Protestant Churchmen. He saw the Anglo-Irish bitterly discontented with the mother country, and the Catholic native Irish regarded by their Protestant oppressors with exactly that combination of intense contempt and loathing, and intense rage and terror, which his American counterpart would have divided between the Negro and the Red Indian. To the Anglo-Irish the native peasant was as loathsome as the first, and as terrible as the second. Even at the close of the century Burke could declare that the various descriptions of the people were kept as much apart as if they were *not only separate nations, but separate species.* There were thousands, he says, who had never talked to a Roman Catholic in their whole lives, unless they happened to talk to a gardener's workman or some other labourer of the second or third order, while a little time before this they were so averse to have them near their persons that they would not employ even those who could never find their way beyond the stables.[1] Chesterfield, a thoroughly impartial and just observer, said in 1764 that the poor people in Ireland were used "worse than negroes" by their masters and the

[1] *Letter to Sir Hercules Langrishe,* Works, ii. 557, *b.*

middlemen.[1] We should never forget that in the transactions with the English Government during the eighteenth century, the people concerned were not the Irish, but the Anglo-Irish, the colonists of 1691, "the aristocracy," as Adam Smith said of them, "not founded in the natural and respectable distinctions of birth and fortune, but in the most odious of all distinctions, those of religious and political prejudices—distinctions which, more than any other, animate both the insolence of the oppressors, and the hatred and indignation of the oppressed."[2]

The directions in which Irish improvement would move, were clear from the middle of the century to men with much less foresight than Burke had. The removal of all commercial restrictions, either by Independence or Union, on the one hand, and the gradual emancipation of the Catholics, on the other, were the two processes to which every consideration of good government manifestly pointed. The first proved a much shorter and simpler process than the second. To the first the only obstacle was the blindness and selfishness of the English merchants. The second had to overcome the virulent opposition of the tyrannical

[1] Earl Stanhope's *History*, v. 123.
[2] Last chapter of the *Wealth of Nations*, p. 430.

Protestant faction in Ireland, the disgraceful but deep-rooted antipathies of the English nation, the weakness of one minister and the Egyptian darkness of his successors, and above all the prejudice of two of the worst and most obstinate of English sovereigns. Burke did not survive to see the fulfilment of either pieces of an Irish policy, of which he was in its general aims one of the earliest and most earnest advocates. The history of the relations between the mother country and her dependency during his life may be characterised as a struggle upon commercial and legislative points, between the Imperial Government and the Anglo-Irish interest, in which each side for its own convenience drew support from the Catholic majority. The efforts to complete the incorporation of Ireland with England by the Government, to procure her independence of England by the Anglo-Irish, lent—not, assuredly, by the design of the workers on either side— powerful succour to the second movement, that which aimed at the restoration of the Catholics to civil rights.

It was easy to see that the resistance of the American colonists would encourage the Anglo-Irish colonists, suffering, as they were, from an identical grievance, to struggle for a similar relief. " To read what was approaching in Ireland in the black and bloody characters of the American war," in Burke's words, became the duty of every enlightened observer of public affairs. Even the King predicted that if America became free, " Ireland would soon follow the same plan, and be a separate state."[1] In fact, along with the American war we had to encounter an Irish war also; but the latter was, as an Irish politician called it at the time, a smothered war. Like the Americans, the Anglo-Irish entered into non-importation compacts, and they interdicted commerce. The Irish volunteers, forty thousand strong, were virtually an army enrolled to overawe the English ministry and Parliament. Following the spirit, if not the actual path, of the Americans, they raised a cry first for commercial, and then for legislative, independence. They were too strong to be resisted, and in 1782 the Irish Parliament acquired the privilege of initiating and conducting its own business, without the sanction or control either of the Privy Council or of the English Parliament. Following a shadow, they missed the substantial reality. Dazzled by the chance of acquiring legislative independence, they had been content with comparatively small commercial concessions obtained by Lord Nugent and Burke in 1778, and with the removal of further restrictions by the alarmed

[1] *Corr. with Lord North*, ii. 254.

minister in the following year. After the concession of their independence in 1782, they found that to procure the abolition of the remaining restrictions on their commerce—the right of trade, for instance, with America and Africa—the consent of the English legislature was as necessary as it had ever been. Pitt, fresh from Adam Smith, brought forward in 1785 his famous commercial propositions, of which the theory was that Irish trade should be free, that Ireland should be admitted to a permanent participation in commercial advantages, while in return for this boon she should, after her hereditary revenue passed a certain point, devote the surplus to purposes, such as the maintenance of the navy, in which both nations had an interest. Nothing could be more equitable, nothing more certain to prove beneficial to the mercantile interest of the sister island. Pitt was to be believed when he declared that of all the objects of his political life, this was in his opinion the most important that he had ever engaged in ; that he did not expect ever to meet another that should rouse every emotion in so strong a degree as this did.[1]

The factious course pursued by the English Opposition was only less detestable than the folly of the Anglo-Irish leaders. Fox, who was ostentatiously ignorant

[1] Earl Stanhope's *Life of Pitt,* i. 261–275.

of political economy, led the charge, first by insisting
that Pitt's measures would annihilate English trade,
would destroy the Navigation Laws, and with them our
maritime strength, and then by turning round and
insisting with as much vehemence as before that they
were an insult to Ireland, and a nefarious attempt to
tamper with her newly gained liberties. Burke followed
his leader.   For once, he materially endangered his
claim to high political integrity.   In 1778 and 1779 he
had nobly resisted the pressure which his mercantile
constituents in Bristol had endeavoured to put upon
him, had warmly supported the Irish claims, and had
lost his seat in consequence.   The precise ground
which he took up in 1785 must not be overlooked, as
it supplies a certain pretext, such as it is, for his abandonment of his former attitude.   He appears to have
discerned in Pitt's proposals the germ of an attempt
to extract revenue from Ireland, identical in purpose
and principle with the memorably disastrous attempt
to extract revenue from America.   Whatever stress we
may lay upon this for the sake of vindicating Burke
from the charge of mere factiousness—a task which
even then we cannot accomplish[1]—we are still com-

[1] Nothing, for example, can be more purely factious than his sneer
at Pitt, in the Speech on the Nabob of Arcot's Debts, for stopping " to

pelled to recognise his inferiority in statesmanship to the minister whom he opposed.

Pitt's alternative was irresistible. Situated as Ireland was, she must either be the subservient instrument of English prosperity, or she must be allowed to enjoy the benefits of English trade, taking, at the same time, a proportionate share of the common burdens.[1] The neighbourhood of Ireland to the shores of the mother country introduced an element into the problem, which must have taught every unimpassioned observer that the American solution would be inadequate for a dependency that lay at our very door. Burke, seeing this, preferred the first alternative, and maintained, in a manner particularly likely to inflame his jealous countrymen, that Irish interests must always inevitably be subordinate to English interests. Yet he lent himself to the party cry that Pitt was taking

pick up chaff and straws" from the Irish revenue, instead of preventing profligate expenditure in India. Works, i. 319, *b.*

[1] Adam Smith had shown that there was nothing incompatible with justice in a contribution by Ireland to the public debt of Great Britain. "That debt has been contracted in support of the government established by the Revolution ; a government to which the Protestants of Ireland owe not only the whole authority which they at present enjoy in their own country, but every security which they possess for their liberty, their property, and their religion."—*Wealth of Nations,* book v. c. iii. p. 430.

his first measures for the re-enslavement of Ireland.
Had it not been for what he himself called the delirium
of the preceding session, and which had still not subsided, he would have seen that Pitt was in truth taking
his first measures for the emancipation of Ireland from
an unjust and oppressive subordination, and for her
installation as a corporate member of the Empire, the
only position permanently possible for her.

That the wise plans of the minister were baffled is
one of the many expressive comments upon the system
of party government.   In 1779 Irish affairs were
happily not a branch of party politics.[1]   The tide ran
higher and covered every inch of ground six years
later.   The Opposition first inflamed English feeling.
In order to conciliate this, Pitt was forced to curtail
the advantages which he had proffered to the Irish
traders.   Then, with this curtailment for one of their
weapons, the Opposition inflamed Irish feeling as they
had before done that of England.   Fox declaimed
shrilly against bartering English commerce for Irish
slavery.   By the time the English had been brought
round to the scheme, the Irish had been thoroughly
alienated from it.   A substantial boon was sacrificed
amid bonfires and candles to the phantom of Irish

[1] *Burke's Works*, ii. 410.

legislative independence. The result must have convinced Pitt more firmly than ever that his great master, Adam Smith, was right in predicting that nothing short of the union of the two countries would deliver Ireland from out of the hands of her fatuous chiefs and their too worthy followers.

If, however, the Anglo-Irish were the victims of the spirit of monopoly in one order, they were its most oppressive organs and ministers in another. America has shown us what a free and noble force Protestantism may develop. Unhappily, at the same moment, Ireland illustrates, in still greater perfection, what a depth of tyrannical cruelty may be engendered in it by opportunity, what a falseness to its own principles, what systematic oppression and inhuman exclusiveness. Protestants love to dwell upon the horrors of the Revocation of the Edict of Nantes, of the proscriptions of Philip II., of the Inquisition. Let them turn candidly to the history of Ireland, from 1691 down to 1798, and they will perceive that the diabolical proscription of the penal laws and the frenzied atrocities with which the Protestants suppressed the Catholic rising at the close of the century, are absolutely unsurpassed in history. The Penal Code has often been transcribed. In a country where the toleration of Protestantism is constantly over-vaunted, it can scarcely be transcribed too often. " It was a system," says Burke, " full of coherence and consistency ; well digested and well composed in all its parts : it was a machine of wise and elaborate contrivance, and as well fitted for the oppression, impoverishment, and degradation of a people, and the debasement in them of human nature itself, as ever proceeded from the perverted ingenuity of man." [1] The creed of the greater part of Christendom was viewed as if it had been the bloody superstition of a tribe of cannibals. To hold the belief which a Bossuet and a Fénelon still lived to adorn while these laws were being conceived, was enough to debar a man from the ordinary privileges of ownership, from sending his children to be educated in his own faith, from the guardianship of his own child if the mother were a Protestant, from marriage with a Protestant if either had any property, from keeping a school, from following the professions of law and physic, and in certain circumstances from the benefit of trial by jury. That these laws were imposed in a moment of rage and panic by a dominant faction is true, and that connivance and indulgence after a long interval began gradually to steal in. The

[1] *Letter to Sir Hercules Langrishe*, Works, i. 560, *b.*

Presbyterian dissenters, also suffering, though in a much slighter measure, from political exclusion, condescended, as the century was drawing to a close, to whisper something about alliance with the Catholics. The English interest, again, and the Irish interest, the two great factions of the dominant race, in their contest for the offices and emoluments of the State, each sought to gain a point against its adversary by tampering with the enemy, whom the one despised and hated as thoroughly as did the other. Slight relaxations were thus obtained by the Irish Catholics in 1774, in 1778, when the English Catholics also were relieved, and in 1782. In 1792, owing partly to the dissensions among the Ascendancy to which I have just referred, and partly, and much more, to the wisdom of Pitt, more important restrictions were removed, and at length in 1793 they nearly all disappeared, those which concerned property long surviving those which were aimed merely at the hostile religion. In the same year also the Catholics were re-admitted to the franchise.

Burke did his best, while he was upon the scene, to accelerate the progress of a large and liberal tolerance. His *Letter to Sir Hercules Langrishe* (1792), upon the propriety of admitting the Catholics to the elective

franchise, is one of the wisest and most completely
satisfactory of all his pieces, so just is its application of history, so enlightened its idea of toleration,
so sagacious its comprehension of political conditions
and exigencies.   Is your government, he asked, likely
to be more secure by continuing causes of grounded
discontent to two-thirds of its subjects?   Will the
Constitution be made more solid by depriving this
large part of the people of all concern or share in its
representation?   We did not destroy the Gallican
Church settlement in Canada, nor rob the Canadian
Catholics of the rights of free subjects.   Turn from
the remote West to the remote East.   The fact that
people in India are Mahometans and Hindoos, and
that the majority of the Christians are Papists, does
not prevent us from undertaking the support of their
rights, privileges, laws, and immunities.   " Thinking
and acting as I have done towards these remote
nations, I should not know how to show my face, here
or in Ireland, if I should say that all the Pagans, all
the Mussulmen, and even all the Papists (since they
must form the highest stage in the climax of evil), are
worthy of a liberal and honourable condition, except
those of one of the descriptions, which forms the
majority of the inhabitants of the country in which

you and I were born. If such are the Catholics of Ireland, ill-natured and unjust people, from our own data, may be inclined not to think better of the Protestants of a soil which is supposed to infuse into its sects a kind of venom unknown in other places." [1]

The sequel of the movement does not fall within Burke's period. As he lay dying, he could observe the tide of angry disaffection and confusion rising and swelling in his native country, until before he had been many months dead, it broke in a tumultuous rebellion that was signalized by horrors on the part of the victorious faction, compared with which the cruelties of his thrice execrated foes, the Jacobins, were almost pardonable. He must be deemed happy in having escaped the most hateful and atrocious episode in English history. The English Government had sown the wind, and it reaped the whirlwind. The process which hatched the Protestant monsters of Lord Cornwallis's time was simple. With the sword and the bayonet we founded a Church in robbery and injustice, we set up an aristocracy on spoils torn from the natives, and then we put into their hands a code of laws wicked enough to expel the last spark of virtue and benevolence from the nature of the very best man

[1] Works, i. 557-560.

o 2

who should have to administer it, or to come within its sphere. If we reflect that this was the seed, we can barely wonder that the fruit has been, and yet remains for us, so passingly bitter.

III. Turning from Ireland to our great dependency in the East, it is easy to see how the circumstances which attended the establishment of English sovereignty in India would affect a statesman of Burke's natural sensibility, profound sympathies with the subjects of government, and active hatred of oppression, injustice, and disorder. Before entering upon a theme of this importance, involving, as it does, a conflict of principle that waxes daily more and more urgent for Englishmen, it is essential that we should settle two fundamental points, or at least, as the next best thing, recognise as clearly as we can that on each of them are held two diametrically opposed sets of views.

First, is it in the present stage of European civilization conducive to the general progress of mankind that any European power should assume the supreme government of a vast nation, with traditions of which we are comparatively ignorant, with ancient institutions that it needs a philosopher to explain or to understand, with wants that we can hardly appreciate, with deep and unalterable peculiarities of character, some of which revolt us, and none of which evoke our sympathy? If we were perfect in probity and virtue, and at the same time adequately armed with intellectual apprehension of the conditions of the problem, and of the means by which to satisfy them, there would be no difficulty in answering the question. /It is impossible to conceive a powerful and enlightened people engaging in any nobler task than that of disinterestedly seeking to impart to a less fortunate and more backward race the acquisitions of their own long effort and experience, in all the moral and intellectual agencies for ameliorating human destiny. / But as yet we are far removed from a state in which such conduct could be anticipated, and this makes it very much more difficult to strike the balance between the advantages and disadvantages of sovereign relations with inferior peoples. Our dealings with India, for example, originally and until Burke's time, so far from being marked with virtue and wisdom, were stained with every vice which can lower and deprave human character. How long will it take only to extirpate these traditions from the recollection of the natives? The more effectually their understandings are awakened by English efforts, the more vividly will they recognise, and the more bitterly resent, the iniquities of our first connexion with them. Among other considerations pointing in the same direction are the distance of the actual governors of the country from the seat of that public opinion to which only they are responsible ; the consequent difficulty of contriving securities for their right conduct ; the improbability of any public opinion existing in the sovereign country itself, at once active enough and well enough informed to operate with good effect ; the small likelihood of the majority of a great body of public servants identifying themselves heartily and energetically with the interests of a country which they think of mostly as a temporary sojourning place on the road to their native country and a pension. Add to these the still graver drawbacks of an indispensable military occupation, and the corrupting effects upon the average representatives of the dominant nation of traditions of conquest, and a never-forgotten superiority of race.

There are, on the other hand, numerous and weighty considerations leading to an opposite conclusion. If we had not made ourselves masters of the country, the struggles for territory and supremacy, which followed upon the death of Aurungzebe and the feebleness of his successors in the Empire—circumstances which have frequently and justly been compared to those of Europe after the death of Charlemagne—would have inflicted greater damage on the growth of India, than it suffered from the iniquitous rapacity of the Company in the earlier days of its power. Again, the improvement in public opinion since the beginning of the present century, both in keenness of interest and in rightness of judgment, has been so rapid and uniform as to justify us in anticipating the very best consequences from its increased operation. This, in turn, will affect the public servants whom we send out; and though it is not likely to inflame them with any ardent patriotism about India, it will lead them more and more to associate their ideas of self-respect and sense of duty with the good government of the people committed to them. Meanwhile, the infiltration of European enlightenment will be taking place by a gradual process, to the manifest advantage of the natives; always provided we can hold our position long enough, and prove its disinterestedness clearly enough, to be able in the end to dispense with an intrusive military force, and to rely simply on such moral sympathy and respect as we may by that time have earned. The final argument on this side, an argument which perhaps conclusively turns the scale, is the fact that we now actually possess supreme power in India, and that if we were to abandon it, from however exalted motives, we should be leaving the country and its inhabitants to disaster and confusion far worse than any we have ever inflicted upon it. It was this last reflection which stifled in the mind of Burke for example, a nascent conviction that it would have been better for us and for India, if Clive had succeeded in his attempt to blow out his own brains in the Madras counting-house, or if the battle of Plassy had been a decisive defeat instead of a decisive victory. "All these circumstances," he once said, in reference to the results of the investigation of the Select Committee, "are not, I confess, very favourable to the idea of our attempting to govern India at all. But there we are : there we are placed by the Sovereign Disposer, and we must do the best we can in our situation. The situation of man is the preceptor of his duty."[1] There is a school of opinion which would accept his aphorism, and would immediately conclude that the duty which our situation enjoins upon us is to leave these backward races to themselves, both for our sake and their own. The majority think otherwise; and so long as they are zealous in seeking, and successful in

[1] *Speech on Fox's East India Bill*, Works, i. 283, b.

finding, high-minded Indian servants, they may do enough in the way of repressing the evils naturally flowing from such a supremacy to justify their own theory about it.

The second question, and practically by far the most important, to which two answers have in like manner been given, is whether, assuming — which certainly nobody thought of doubting a century since — that supremacy over an inferior people is good for Europeans, the superior race is bound to observe the highest current morality of the time, in all their dealings with the subject race. Or, does the end, justifying the means, entitle us to sink upon occasion to the lower level of their morality? Have moral considerations, again, any place in political transactions; or are we to learn that though it is atrocious for a man to cheat, lie, and murder for his personal profit, these actions become harmless or even laudable when they are committed for the benefit of a government or a corporation? Is a European under any obligation to respect the rights and immunities of an Asiatic, if he have physical force enough to defeat them; or is an Asiatic incapable of rights? Finally, is there some peculiarity about wilful cruelty, rapine, and lawlessness in cold blood, when practised for political ends and towards inferior races, which preserves the character of the perpetrator from any contagion from his acts, and disentitles us from stigmatising him as cruel, rapacious, and an oppressor ?

The way in which we answer this set of questions determines our attitude in criticising Burke's policy in the affairs of India. If we answer them in one way, Burke will figure in our eyes as a virulent and fanatical dreamer ; if in another, we shall revere him as the first apostle and great upholder of integrity, humanity, and honour in the relations between his countrymen and their Indian subjects. If we believe that Clive was justified in tricking Omichund by forging another man's name ; that Impey was justified in hanging Nuncomar for committing the very offence for which Clive was excused or applauded, although forgery is no grave crime according to Hindoo usage, and it is the gravest according to English usage ; that Hastings was justified in selling English troops to assist in the extermination of a brave people with whom he was at peace ; that Benfield was justified in conniving with an Eastern prince in a project of extortion against his subjects,— if our indulgence is due to the policy of which these were faint illustrations, then we may set down Burke as a troublesome declaimer, a narrow-minded and cavilling

politician. If, on the other hand, we conceive all this
to have been the deepest stain which the honour and
repute of the English Government has ever received,
and to have been hardly atoned for by the benevolence
and usefulness of our subsequent dealings, we shall
know how much we owe to the unwearied labours of
the statesman who exposed the crimes of the offenders,
and taught the governing race the duties of beneficence.

It is sometimes said that Burke's sympathies were
blindly misplaced; that the princes, and begums, and
aged ministers, whose illustrious rank and oriental
pomp are supposed to have kindled his eager imagination, were in truth the chief centres of oppression
and misery for their millions of subjects. This kind
of argument may have weight in the mouths of the
annexationists of a later time. In the time of Clive
and Hastings, the hand of the Europeans fell heavily
upon princes, but more often it fell heavily upon the
wretched natives through the princes. The necessity
of complying with the exactions of the Company
caused the demands of the princes upon their unfortunate subjects to be more excessive and relentless
than they had ever been before. Besides, some of
those transactions which Burke assailed most vehemently, cannot by any ingenuity be represented as

merciful to subjects, while oppressive only to princes. Consider the case of the Rohilla War. A greedy and cowardly Nabob of Oude thirsted to annex the rich region of Rohilcund to his own dominions, but the Rohillas who possessed it were brave and hardy. He knew that by his troops they were invincible, so he paid Hastings four hundred thousand pounds for the loan of an English brigade and an English colonel, whom he employed to crush a valiant people, without provocation, and without mercy. Can any Englishman who loves his country, read of this execrable crime, even at this distance, without feeling his ears tingle for shame ? After English troops had put the Rohillas to flight, the whole district was overspread with the flames of burning villages, and our soldiers had, with suppressed murmurs, to watch their allies engaged in scenes which the English commander would not trust himself to describe. A partisan historian insists that the war was against the Rohilla chiefs, who were military adventurers, and not against the people. Yet we have the testimony of eye-witnesses to the ruin which overtook the people, the cruelty with which they were driven from their homes, and the desolation which reigned over a once prosperous country. When these atrocities were represented to

Hastings, he replied, with incomparable self-possession, that they were usual in Eastern warfare, and, what was more, that the English, when at war with this very Nabob of Oude ten years before, had burnt and ravaged his country in the same way in which he was burning and ravaging the country of the Rohillas.[1] War cannot be made with rose-water, but it will scarcely be pretended that a governor lending his troops for a sum of money to another ruler, who with their indirect aid overruns a whole district with fire and sword, deserves credit for protecting a suffering population against rapacious sovereigns.

Another of the transactions which Burke was equally active in discovering and denouncing, and which it is equally impossible to explain away by urging that he was misled as to the rightful object of his sympathy, was the famous fraud of the Nabob of Arcot's Debts. Benfield, an obscure servant of the Company at

---

[1] Wilson's note to Mill's *British India*, vol. iii. p. 403 (fifth edition). The assurance with which Wilson tells us that the war was not against the people, with Colonel Champion's own words before him on the page, is one of the most marvellous exhibitions in that most irritating piece of editing. The love of contradicting his author, of assailing him for want of candour, for misrepresentation, for political economy, for utilitarianism, seem to have absolutely blinded the editor to anything like morality, and sometimes to anything like common sense.

Madras, found means to lend this personage, or to
pretend to lend him, some small sum, at an extortionate
rate of interest.   Interest was accumulated upon interest, and principal upon principal, until the total
demand reached the enormous sum of two hundred
and thirty-four thousand pounds.   There were other
claims of the same sort, amounting in all to some
millions.   Forbidden to take presents, the servants of
the Company made fictitious loans, repayable by assign-
ments on the public revenue.   If their private claims
had been a question between the Nabob and the
creditors, Burke confessed that he would not have
stirred.   Meeting by anticipation the position sometimes taken up now, he declared that if the demands
were confined to what might be drawn from hoarded
treasures alleged to be in the Nabob's possession, the
creditors might freely break open his hoards, and dig
in his mines without disturbance.   But the Nabob
and his creditors were collusive parties.   The litigation
was not, nor ever had been, between their rapacity and
his riches.   No, it was " between him and them combining and confederating on one side, and the public
revenues and the miserable inhabitants of a ruined
country on the other.   It is, therefore, not from treasuries and mines, but from the food of your unpaid

armies, from the blood withheld from the veins, and whipt out of the backs of the most miserable of men, that we are to pamper extortions, usury, and peculation, under the false names of debtors and creditors of State."[1]

It is not only in these two conspicuous cases, but throughout all his speeches and writings upon the subject of India, that we may see how clear-sighted, as well as how genuine, was Burke's abhorrence of the general character of European relations in the East. It must be observed that the crimes which he attacked were not the unfortunate, but often excusable, excesses of military heat. They sprung not from panic, but from policy. They were dictated not by strategical necessity, but by a colossal cupidity. They not only effected the humiliation of Rajahs and Nabobs, and the deposition of august oppressors, but they aggravated the sufferings of the oppressed, and plunged the wretched millions into a misery more than oriental. What Burke's sensitive imagination fixed upon was not the woes of a sovereign despoiled of gold and silver, of silks and jewels, but the merciless hand that "tore the cloth from the loom, or wrested the scanty portion of rice and salt from the peasant of Bengal,

[1] Works, i. 322, *b.* Mill's *British India,* iv. 89, and v. 21-30.

or wrung from him the very opium in which he forgot his oppressions and his oppressors." It is possible that he may have estimated more highly than truth would warrant the prosperity and well-being of the inhabitants of Hindustan before the arrival of European traders and the first encroachments of the English. He could not exaggerate the sufferings inflicted by conquerors who came, not like the ancient conquerors, to find a home and organize a settlement, but avowedly to wring what they could from the natives, and then, after they had done their best to rifle the country, to leave it for new-comers yet further to exhaust. If ever a single-minded and righteous anger burned in the breast of man, it was in the case of Edmund Burke as he reflected on the wrongs and miseries of the natives of India. If a revolution took place in the whole spirit of the English government, it was due to the weight of that more generous public opinion which he did more to create than any one else before or since.

Plunder in three forms, and diverted into three channels, was the very *raison d'être* of the power of the Company. First, the proprietors of East India stock clamoured for dividends. Secondly, the State insisted on an annual payment of four hundred thousand pounds as the price of the privileges which the Company enjoyed. Thirdly, the public servants went out penniless, intending to return, and actually returning, with immense fortunes. Each of these three claims had to be satisfied. The claim of the State, greedy and unconsidered as it was, still was capable of being measured, but the other two were infinite and unfathomable. The desires of the Company and its servants were absolutely insatiable, and could only be limited by the last pagoda and the last piece of silk in the country. The servants, being on the spot, were in truth the masters. The greater the private emoluments of the servants, the lower sank the fortunes of the Company. Men became proprietors of stock, that they might either themselves acquire posts, or might procure a post for a son or a nephew. The advantage sought was not interest upon capital, not dividend upon shares, but participation in patronage,—immediate in the case of a director, indirect in the case of a proprietor.[1] Or else, men sought votes in order, by supporting some servant in India against hostile motions, to earn a portion of the spoils which he scattered broadcast on his return home.[2] The Minister

[1] *Ninth Report*, Burke's Works, ii. 3, *a.* Mill's *British India*, iii. 355.
[2] *Speech on Fox's India Bill*, Works, i. 297, *b.*

P

had only such control over the Directors as he could acquire obliquely, by votes purchased more or less overtly by a place in the Treasury or the Ordnance Office. The Directors had a very imperfect control, or even no control at all, over servants who were many thousand miles away from Leadenhall Street, and in corresponding with whom it took a year or more to send a despatch and receive a reply. Practically, therefore, until 1783, India was governed irresponsibly. There was not even the minor guarantee of responsibility, not to the governed nation, but to the governing nation at home. If some of the presidential governors had had the power, a mere instinctive dislike of rapacity and disorder might have driven them to restrain their subordinates. But they were paralysed. Pigot, for example, was rendered powerless against Benfield by his own council. Hastings, again, like Clive, had no doubt an innate preference for good government, but his political pre-occupations left him little time for watching or restraining those who imitated his own misdeeds, on a pettier scale in a less conspicuous station.[1]

[1] See *Lord Cornwallis's Corr.* i. 227, where he says that the grossest frauds had been daily committed before the faces of the late Government.

The nature even of the more legitimate and acknowledged commercial transactions was as ruinous for the natives as it is possible to conceive. Readers of the history of the Company are familiar with the name of the Investment. What was this ? Simply a portion of the revenues of Bengal set aside every year, for the purchase of goods to be exported to England. This, it is sufficiently clear, was not commerce at all, but only an exaction of tribute by a double, instead of by a single, process. The English first took money, then they changed the money for goods. This was in effect just as if they had extorted the goods in the first instance, except that in this case there would have been no delusion in the minds of people at home as to the existence of a commerce, in which the natives were believed to be thriving. As it is stated in the Ninth Report of the Select Committee—one of the most luminous and exhaustive of English state papers —"the whole exported produce of the country (so far as the Company is concerned) is not exchanged in the course of barter, but is taken away without any return or payment whatsoever : in a commercial light, therefore, England becomes annually bankrupt to Bengal to the amount nearly of its own dealing ; or rather, the country has suffered what is tantamount to

an annual plunder of its manufactures and its produce to the value of twelve hundred thousand
pounds."[1]

This is only a single illustration of the flat and
undisguised selfishness of our early intercourse with
Asiatics.   Besides the produce of the Investment, every
ship that sailed carried away the goods in which private
individuals transmitted their private gains, procured
with even less justice than the Investment itself from
the natives, and without a shadow or pretence of a
return.   As Burke finely said, "The cries of India were
given to seas and winds to be blown about, in every
breaking up of the monsoon, over a remote and un-
hearing ocean."   If the reader desires to convince himself further of that mass of fraud, peculation, collusion,
in all their complex involutions, which then constituted
the government of India, let him turn to the Ninth
Report, or to the correspondence of Lord Cornwallis ;
who, first as Governor-General of India immediately
after Pitt's reform, and then as Lord-Lieutenant of
Ireland during the Rebellion, was destined to see in
the West and the East alike, how vile the nature of
his countrymen could become.

There was, it need scarcely be said, no attempt to

[1] *Burke's Works,* ii. 14, *a.*

understand the previous history of the country, to realise the spirit of its laws and usages, to take up the thread of its progress, and so to work out a rational and orderly course of evolution. Justice was administered in Bengal as if it had been Wiltshire or Essex. The rules and procedure of an English court were transplanted to a land inhabited by Mahometans and Hindoos, and without the English safeguards against oppression or misunderstanding. The uncouth and rigid forms in which English jurisprudence has clothed itself, were stretched and distorted to cover cases, to which their adaptation was wholly impracticable. The courts were more terrible to the native than the worst wrongs which they pretended to redress. The customs and laws and moral ideas of the country were spurned with disdain by men, who were ignorant of the irreparable mischief they were doing, in neglecting the only foundations on which it was possible to erect a durable social superstructure. Scorning the past they ruined the future. Burke might well declare himself stupified by " the desperate boldness of a few young men, who having obtained a power of which they saw neither the purposes nor the limits, tossed about, subverted, and tore to pieces, as if it were in the gambols of a boyish unluckiness and malice, the most established rights and the most ancient and most revered institutions of ages and nations."

Ingenious apologists assure us with impressive gravity, that the Company and its servants were not any more cruel and greedy than the native princes. If they are content that Europeans in the latter half of the eighteenth century should only be no worse than barbarians, this protest is perfectly adequate. Burke's action was taken, and enlightened modern opinion rests, upon the pardonable hypothesis that Europeans ought not only to have been less tyrannical, perfidious, and destructive, than barbarous rajahs, but not to have been tyrannical and perfidious at all.

The admiration that we are invited to give to Hastings and Clive for the imposing achievements which they effected, might have been due if their success had been attained without any sacrifice of honour or humanity. But let us suspect the men who never reach good except through evil. A great statesman of later times exclaimed, that anybody can govern with a state of siege. In the same way, any man of thoroughly inferior capacity could conquer any nation of crafty and cruel barbarians, if he is permitted, with the superior material forces which a more advanced civilization puts into his hand, to stoop to all violence or perfidy from which his enemies would not shrink. The triumph of men in the situation of Hastings would be just and admirable, if they achieved their aims without the unscrupulous sacrifice of humane and upright principle. With this sacrifice, it is a victory won not by the finest, but by the coarsest qualities of human nature. And even by the vulgar measurement of temporary results, these victories of violence are egregiously overvalued. They are scarcely ever more than temporary makeshifts. The real work, the latent but not less insuperable difficulties against which violence is futile, have to be encountered afterwards by men of essentially greater capacity than the hero who dazzles his contemporaries with showy and truculent exploits. Thus from the lowest point of view which any considerations of mere policy, not professedly of the hour or the day, present, scrupulous honour and humanity would in the long run have been more successful, than any of those triumphs for which we paid so costly a price in the good name of our nation.

We find a writer of sound judgment and a singularly high sense of national honour, like Macaulay, confessing that his hero had laid it down as an axiom, a proposition beyond examination or dispute, that when he had not as much money as the public service required, he was to take it from anybody who had ; that he was a man of lax principles and a hard heart ; that he did not respect the rights nor sympathise with the sufferings of others. Are valour, intrepidity, quick shiftiness, then, to be put into the opposite scale, and to outweigh these criminal characteristics? Hastings was disinterested, it is true. He was not a vulgar freebooter, like the men who plundered India before his face. But the question in Burke's time was whether oppression and corruption were to continue to be the guiding maxims of English policy. The personal disinterestedness of the ruler who had been the chief founder of this policy, who had most openly set aside all pretence of righteous principle, surely was mere dust in the balance. It was impossible to suppress the policy without striking a deadly blow at its main instrument, its most eminent and powerful organ. That Hastings was acquitted was immaterial. The lesson of his impeachment had been taught with sufficient force—the great lesson that Asiatics have rights, and that Europeans have obligations ; and that the authority of the English legislature is not more entirely a trust for the benefit of this country, than the dominion of the English in India is a trust for the benefit of the inhabitants of India.[1]

Besides the great modification of fundamental ideas with reference to India which had been effected by the proceedings against Hastings, and in which Burke took the leading part, he was active in another highly important change. The Reports of the various select committees upon Indian affairs—the most important of them all, the ninth and the eleventh, being drawn up by Burke himself—had shown conclusively that the existing system of government was thoroughly corrupt and thoroughly inadequate. Hence the introduction of Fox's famous India Bill, and immediately after its memorable rejection by the exertion of the royal influence in the House of Lords, the introduction and enactment of Pitt's India Bill.[2] The provisions of

[1] The case against the impeachment may be found stated with force in Wilson's note to Mill's *British India*, v. 194-200. The writer admits that Hastings exhibited some slight errors and imperfections ; but " the answer to this is—he was a man." In the same astounding spirit of tolerance, the editor rebukes his author for assailing the old unreformed parliament, and attributes its defects, such as they were, simply " to the bounded extent of human wisdom and virtue." (iv. 389.)

[2] It is now ascertained pretty conclusively that the India Bill of the Coalition was conceived and drawn by Burke, and that he deserves whatever merit or demerit belongs to it. (Cf. Sir G. C. Lewis's *Administrations of Great Britain*, pp. 99-101.)

these two measures have been so often described—of the first, in detailing the parliamentary struggle to which it gave rise ; of the second, as the actual instrument of Indian government for seventy years—that I need not dwell upon them.[1]

On one point there exists a misconception which is worth correcting. The historians all seem to have the impression, that the Bill which became law was not much else than a slightly modified copy of the Bill which had been thrown out in the previous year, to the general satisfaction of the public, who hated it as the work of the unpopular Coalition. In matters of immediate administrative detail, indeed, the provisions of the one were substantially those of the other also. As the historian of British India shows, the first measure, in this part of it, aimed at little else than a prohibition for the future of the various specific delinquencies which had been discovered in the past. The author of the second measure, therefore, proposing nothing higher or more comprehensive than this, in forbidding the same offences necessarily introduced similar clauses. But if we look at those portions of the two schemes defining the nature of the systems of

[1] See Mill's *British India*, iv. 381–412. Massey's *History of England*, iii. 61, and 111. Stanhope's *Life of Pitt*, i. 138.

government which they respectively propose, we shall perceive a striking distinction in the ideas on which they are founded, and an organic difference of principle. Fox's Bill handed over the government of India to a Board chosen by the House of Commons—to a branch, in fact, of its own executive, and responsible to the legislature, just as the Admiralty or Ordnance Boards were. Pitt's Bill, on the other hand, left the government in the hands of the Directors, a body with the special knowledge and special experience required for the right administration of a remote and peculiar dependency, while he set over them a second body with rights of inspection and prohibition. There is thus just the difference in principle between these two schemes, that there is between our present system and that which, after the Indian Mutiny, it superseded.

In 1858 we found India governed directly by a permanent executive, which did not change with the various ministries of the day, but was only subject to a certain supervision from them. We found a delegated body with every opportunity for knowing India, as only long experience and exclusive attention could enable men to know it, and we found a Board of Control changing its chief with the ministry, and so from time to time giving the real executive the benefit of a fresh mind and new ideas, from the outside of their own special grooves. This was the system of double government which Pitt and Dundas set up in 1784. Its cardinal distinction is the commission of executive duties to a permanent body, not directly amenable to the votes or the public opinion of the House of Commons. The cardinal distinction of Fox's Bill was the withdrawal of power from the permanent and trained body, and its transfer to the nominees of Parliament.

Burke was so convinced of the incurable iniquity of the Company, so persuaded that it was not only full of abuses, but, as he said, one of the most corrupt and destructive tyrannies that probably ever existed in the world, as to be content with nothing short of the absolute deprivation of its power. He avowed himself no lover of names, and that he only contended for good government, from whatever quarter it might come. But the idea of good government coming from the Company he declared to be desperate and untenable. This intense animosity, which, considering his long and close familiarity with the infamies of the rule of the Company's servants, was not unnatural, must be allowed, however, to have blinded him to the grave objections which really existed to his scheme. In the first place, the Bill was indisputably inconsistent with the spirit of his revered Constitution. For the legislature to assume the power of naming the members of an executive body was an extraordinary and mischievous innovation. Then, to put patronage, which has been estimated by a sober authority at about three hundred thousand pounds a year, into the hands of the House of Commons was an amazing feat. After a certain time, again, the nomination of the Commissioners would fall to the Crown, and this might in certain contingencies increase the ascendancy of the royal authority to a most dangerous extent. But more interesting, to us at least, than these objections from the constitutional point of view, is the consideration of the effect of the measure upon the country most directly and deeply concerned. There are two things to be said against the continuance of power in the hands of the Company. They had shown themselves at once avaricious and incompetent in the past ; and there was no reason to believe that they would cease to rule the country by methods of routine and with a view to their own interests, for the future. Two arguments, on the other side, seem still more cogent ; first, the danger of entrusting the government of such a continent as India to seven men who knew

nothing special about it; next, the danger of removing
from over the subject population the only authority
they had been accustomed to obey, and to identify
with English superiority. That is, in a word, if we
abolished the government by the Directors, there
was the danger arising from the inexperience and
strangeness of their successors; if we retained it,
there was the not inferior danger of routine and traditional corruption.

The chief aim in any system for governing a people,
so much behind ourselves as the natives of Hindustan,
must certainly be to get the various administrative
posts filled by men of trained skill and of the highest
character that the governing people can produce. The
disposal of patronage, therefore, was the process which
needed to be most anxiously watched. If Burke's
measure had been carried, the patronage would have
been transferred to a body much less competent than
the Directors to judge of the qualities required in
the fulfilment of this or that administrative charge.
Indian promotion would have followed parliamentary
and party interest. In the hands of the Directors there
was at least a partial security, in their professional
knowledge and their personal interest in the success of
their government, that places would not be given away

on irrelevant considerations. Their system, with all
its faults, insured the acquisition of a certain considerable competency in administration, before a servant
reached an elevation at which he could do much harm.
Dundas, though unconsciously, no doubt—for he never
in any circumstances exhibited the least aversion to
jobbing places—thus preserved an element which at
that day, at all events, it was highly desirable to preserve, and which even now eminent publicists think us
rash in having discarded.

If it was thus desirable to leave the ordinary
patronage in the hands of a special and intermediate
body, with peculiar qualifications for knowing the conditions and demands of the country to be governed,
it was equally desirable that the main post of all should
be bestowed on some one, who should owe a direct
allegiance and responsibility to the imperial executive.
While enjoying all the benefits of a trained body of
advisers, in the servants by whom he was surrounded,
he would bring to the administration a mind unem-
barrassed by special traditions, and free from irregular
personal or local preferences. The appointment of this
high officer away from the service would have been
as possible under Burke's scheme, as it was in that of
Dundas.

One more remark remains. In considering the American Revolution, we came across one of the elements which prepared that extraordinary endurance of absolutism, repression, and reaction, which astonishes the reader of English history from the Revolution down to the Reform Bill. The tyrannical ideas which sprung up among all classes during the American War demoralised public opinion. We may find another element in the feeling which gradually arose during the too prolonged trial of Hastings. By the end of the trial the delinquent had not only the court and the clergy on his side—that alliance was natural and unfailing—but the general public opinion of the country. The proceedings had familiarized people with acts and ideas of oppression. It is one of the most significant characteristics of lawlessness that, like the most deadly diseases, it is infectious. India was for many years a chief forcing-house, whence arbitrary notions of the most pestilent sort were transplanted into England. This was only the necessary reaction of an arbitrary and selfish policy—not the least of the evils which such a policy entails.

CHAPTER VI.

THE FRENCH REVOLUTION.

THE establishment of Catholicism, the Reformation, and the Revolution, mark three great stages through which the mind of Europe has travelled since the decline of the Western Empire. Each of these names covers a set of moral and intellectual conceptions, in which are contained the germs of some of the chief social changes, that have transformed Europe from its state in the fourth century, to its state in the nineteenth, and all three of which are still working in the accomplishment of a further and more radical transformation. The history of the process by which one of these systems of belief has gradually been made to give way in the most far-seeing minds to its successor, would be the history of the Renaissance, of the development of speculative philosophy, of the advance of physical science, in a word, of the evolution of ideas in every order of thought which, directly and indirectly, is able to modify man's con-

victions about the relations between himself and all
that lies beyond himself.   Though each has had a
special geographical centre, Catholicism in Italy, the
Reformation in Germany, the Revolution in France,
the movement has in each case extended with varying
strength and in different forms over the rest of the
European federation.   With a common organization
lying in the background of our past history, and with
a constant and close communication, it is impossible
that powerful progressive elements in one nation should
not, with some modifications in their embodiment, exercise an energetic influence over the other members of
the same general body.

There is an important distinction in the nature of
the exact connexion between the several movements.
The Reformation, while adding something to Catholicism in the shape of dogma, and stripping it of much
in the matter of discipline, still must be acknowledged
to have sprung from the bosom, and to have been
tended by the sons, of Catholicism.   The Revolution,
though deeply indebted to the Protestant armoury for
many weapons which helped to clear the way, and to
Jansenism, which was Protestant doctrine with Catholic
discipline, still arose from springs, and flowed in a
channel, of its own.   Contrasted with the Revolution,

the Reformation remained of close kith and kin with Catholicism. Again, the order of influence is somewhat different. The Reformation had its roots in spiritual needs and theological diversities, and only led indirectly to momentous political changes. The Revolution, in its primary aspect almost purely political, only subsequently reveals its profound moral and spiritual bearings. The Reformation, emancipating the minds of those who were ripe for it from heavy spiritual burdens, contributed also, as Holland, England, and America showed, to engender a strong desire for political emancipation. The Revolution, in its earlier stages the offspring of material disorder and the organ of secular reform, soon became a tremendous engine of spiritual regeneration, to whose power even yet the world fails to render perfect justice.

For, above all things, let us never forget that those manifold agencies which are summed up under the name of the Revolution, are still at work. The Treaties of Vienna were not to the Revolution, what the Peace of Westphalia was to the Reformation. Whether we look upon the Revolution merely as the final destroyer of systems of social privilege and spiritual authority, previously all but worn out, or, more than this, as contributing permanent and positive elements to human progress, we must in either case perceive that its forces were not exhausted nor its activity terminated, with the Empire, or at the restoration of the old dynasty to the French throne. The history of Europe since the Treaties of Vienna has been little else than the history of their abrogation; in other words, of the revival and spread of that Revolution which they were believed to have finally quelled. Old dynasties, old divisions of classes, old forms of privileged government survive, but little political foresight is needed to disclose that they are all doomed, and that they are only endured as temporary resting-places on an onward road. The conception of finality and equilibrium might seem to have vanished from the midst of every nation in Europe. Every statesman recognises more or less frankly the transitory character of the system which he for the hour administers and upholds. Everywhere we discern the hand and hearken to the tread of the Revolution.

To insist upon identifying this general and continuous movement with the first phase of it, is as misleading and as inadequate as it would be to conceive the Reformation as covered and wholly comprehended in the single history of Luther or of Calvin, of Cranmer or of Knox. In considering the successive

epochs of the French Revolution,—for we may speak
of the rapidly crowded transactions of these eight or
ten years as if they extended over many generations,
as indeed in a sense they are doing,—it is our constant
business to separate in them that which was accident
of time or place or person, from that which belonged
to the spirit and essence of the movement. Each
aspect of it claims investigation and thought ; but in
watching the sets of events as they followed one
another with impetuous haste, let us beware of putting
a finger upon this set or that,—upon the acts of the
Constituent Assembly, of the Commune, of the Legislative, of the Convention ; upon the fall of the Bastille,
or the death of the King, or the Terror ; upon Mirabeau
or Marat, upon Danton or Robespierre,—and exclaiming
that here then was the Revolution. The more atten-
tively we study the character of the chiefs who came to
the surface and then swiftly disappeared, and the more
thoroughly we grasp the meaning of those situations,
each of which seems to be so critical and decisive,
the more irresistibly is the conviction borne in upon
us that the spirit of the Revolution was something
above all these and beside them. Would the King in
exile have been more dangerous than was the spectre
of the King guillotined ? If Mirabeau had lived,

would he by some constitutional system have gratified the passion of the nation and at the same time have soothed the fears and pride of the King and Queen? Or was his design first to level all distinctions of rank and class, to abolish privileges, to destroy local franchises, immunities, and usages, and thus by equalizing all else to leave the royal power supreme, with himself to play the part of Richelieu? What was the secret of the weakness and fall of the Girondins? What is the true theory of the Terror, or are we to believe that it was a mere insane outbreak of cruel frenzy? Under what influences did the ideas of the political structure raised by the Convention fall away before Napoleon? There are a hundred questions of this kind, questions of the deepest historic interest and instruction. Apart, in the background of them all, and overshadowing them all, moves a gigantic, impalpable, impersonal spirit, the Revolution.

It is often regretted by the liberal thinkers of England and of Italy, that circumstances brought the great European movement of the eighteenth century to a head in France, rather than in some other country. The French, it is said, were not prepared. Sunk in despotism, how should they know the uses and conditions of liberty? It would be fairer, as it seems to me, to attribute the disastrous failure of the Revolution in France, not so much to her unfitness for liberty, as to the still more imperfect preparation of her neighbours. It was the enmity of the retrograde powers of Europe which first drove her into the excesses natural to panic, and then by their flagitious designs aroused that military temper, which eventually slew her newborn freedom. The early simplicity and ignorance of the outside world which made the first movers in the Revolution suppose that other nations would rejoice with France over her newly-gotten gifts, was in one sense a token of unpreparedness. But all the circumstances connected with it are marked with that kind of indiscretion which is single-minded, generous, and even touching. Historians appear to be more and more agreed that it was the repulse of this spirit, together with the attitude taken by the continental sovereigns, which filled the nation first with anger, and then with an ever-present, irrational, and as Mr. Carlyle has called it, absolutely preternatural, suspicion.

The researches of philosophers have shown abundantly why it was that the inevitable outbreak of the century which had been prefigured by unmistakeable signs, like the abolition of the Order of Jesuits, the attempted reforms of Joseph II., and numberless other

incidents of equal significance, took place in France
rather than elsewhere. De Tocqueville's work on the
Ancient Régime proves that the condition of the French
population was not worse, but better, than that of the
rest of continental Europe, and that it was this very
superiority which made them chafe more restlessly
against the relics of feudal privileges. It was the
alleviation of the burdens, which made them seem so
intolerable. The old régime had been more strikingly
reformed in the districts round Paris than elsewhere,
while it pressed with unaltered weight upon Brittany,
yet Paris was the heart of the Revolution, and Brittany
its hottest enemy. He proves next that the system of
centralization, which has been usually believed, alike
by those who love it and those who hate it, to be the
product of the Revolution, was in truth the very key-
stone of the old system of administration, and that
this, among other effects, gave an important predominance to the capital city which you could find in no
other state—a predominance big with consequences for
the nation. Again, the literary class in France, unlike
the purely studious German on the one hand, and the
mixed political and practical character of the man of
letters in England on the other, were not purely speculative, while still the institutions of the old régime

prevented them from actually participating in public life. The activity of the members of this class, their brightness, their alluring enthusiasm for symmetry and simplicity in social arrangements, all helped to put into their hands the only educational power in the country, until the whole people, down to women and peasants, as De Tocqueville says, were penetrated with ideas about society and humanity.[1] As neither the people nor their literary instructors had the slightest intimacy with the practical conditions and difficulties of government, and yet were filled with inspiring ideals, the mischief which came of the attempt of these too finished novices to modify an ancient and complex fabric might have been foreseen. The aristocracy, on the other hand, stripped of all powers and destitute of any appointed duties, yet clad in privileges and immunities, and walking in all the stolid pride of caste, between the jealousy of the crown and the hatred of their inferiors were left in a state of isolation and consequent weakness, which has had no parallel in the

---

[1] Is it not one reason why France became revolutionary earlier than any other country, that some of the most powerful sceptical solvents were supplied there, not by the learned for the learned, but by popular writers like Rabelais, Montaigne, and Molière ?

For examples of the cloud of brochures which fell like snow over France at the elections of '89, see Chassin's *Génie de la Révolution*, i. c. 6.

history of any similar body. The manner in which Louis XVI. proclaimed his reforms, and the persistency with which he kept bringing reform forward, was another reason why his subjects rather than those of another should be filled with fatal restlessness. Besides, on more than one occasion, borrowing some of the most levelling phrases of the philosophers, he habitually invited revolution by an ostentatious deference to public opinion, which stands out in strong contrast to the autocratic and irresponsible style of royal reformers in other countries. Then, again, upon the imagination of no other people was the rise of the American republic likely to make so deep an impression. The French Government had lent practical aid to the rebellious colonists. Men like Franklin and Jefferson exerted a perceptible influence over the society of Paris, and especially over some of the earliest popular leaders. The prominence of La Fayette in the opening act of the drama, testifies that it was the altar of American liberty at which the revolutionary torch was first kindled, though it was soon seized by men who worshipped a new and strange goddess of their own. As we meditate on these and other reasons why the uprising against continued imprisonment in the bonds of the Middle Age took place in France rather than elsewhere, we may see that some of these reasons point also, in a certain sense, to her peculiar fitness for the critical task which had fallen upon her.

The writers who maintain that the movement of the eighteenth century was already developing the most useful and admirable reforms, and would have given to Europe all the gifts which the Revolution is ever destined to give, both more speedily and more securely, and without its miseries, seem not perfectly to appreciate the *idées-mères* of the events which they so bitterly and speciously deplore. It is quite true that very improved ideas of good government had grown up in the minds of European rulers before 1789. The reign of Charles III. in Spain marks the most beneficent period in the history of that country. In Prussia, Frederick II. had devoted all that part of his life which was not occupied in the territorial consolidation of his kingdom, to vigorous assaults upon administrative abuses, and to energetic efforts to plant wise laws and usages throughout his dominions. In Austria and the Netherlands, Joseph II., though succeeding in nothing, as he said of himself, and ever taking the second step before he had taken the first, as Frederick said of him, had still attempted everything. His brother Leopold, with greater caution and wisdom, but

with equal zeal, had made Tuscany the happiest part
of Europe.   In England, Pitt was labouring successfully against a factious Opposition and a stupid King
to relieve commerce and the colonies, to enlarge toleration, and to loosen the hold of the slave interest.   In
France itself had there not been a Turgot ?

The wise schemes associated with the names of all
these reformers we are bound to recognise, but we
must also perceive that, while they moved in one
path, the ideas of the Revolution marched in another
and a very different track, leading to a state and to the
embodiment of principles with which Joseph and
Leopold, Charles III. and Frederick II., could, from
their position and training, have no real sympathy.
The question was not merely one of good government
or bad.   It was something much deeper than the better
administration of the laws, the composition of a code,
a fiscal reform, the establishment of civil equality.
M. Quinet has shown, with great force,[1] that the
material, social, territorial, revolution was consummated
when the King gave his consent to the sweeping
measures of the famous Fourth of August,—the Night
of Pentecost, it has been called, according to the
Church of Jean Jacques.   Privilege and immunity

[1] *La Révolution*, vol. i. book 4.

were then cut up, root and branch, by the nominally united will of nobles, clergy, and third estate, within three weeks after the fall of the Bastille. And, indeed, did not the attack on the Bastille itself· portend a change with other than material objects ? The besiegers who surged forth from the Faubourg Saint-Antoine, had no grudge against the State prison. Their punishment was not the duress of stone walls and iron bars, but to be hanged on forty-feet gallows. The Fourteenth of July was the insurrection of an idea, and, as this, it was the first step in a revolution of ideas.

The royal *avant-couriers* of the Revolution, as they are quaintly but not very justly called, had none of those conceptions which since '89 have formed the alphabet of European politics. They had not, they could not have, the fundamental conception of all, that a new and mighty current had arisen in affairs, before which not only administrative forms and fiscal ordinances were to be forced to amend themselves, but which was to overturn the whole existing fabric from its lowest foundations. There had been immense reforms within the pale of Catholicism before Luther, but they were impotent to effect a change, comparable in kind with the consequences to Northern Europe of the Reformation. Does not as much hang upon the

vital spirit in which a great alteration is wrought,
as upon its palpable and ponderable results? The
French Revolution, which was the first event to
announce the ultimate and inevitable overturn, proved,
owing to the operation of causes whch did not lie too
far beneath the surface, a practical failure in most of
its local and subordinate aspects.   Nevertheless, it
sounded over Europe a piercing trumpet-note.   It
was the signal of doom for the cumbersome and obso-
lete sovereignty of the aristocratic and ecclesiastical
system of the Middle Age, already tottering and
hollow.   This was a strange thing in the ears of the
most sagacious and earnest of the administrative
reformers.   Their object had been of another and a
humbler kind.   The physician may repair and amelio-
rate a worn-out system : the Revolutionists, like Medea
with Æson, used the knife and the fiery cauldron
with aspirations not of repair, but of renewal, not of
reform, but of new birth.   They failed, but their aspiration became immortal.   Their failure, miserable and
terrible as it has been, could not obliterate the memory
of their first hope and lesson, that the transfiguration
of old Europe will one day accomplish itself from the
very roots upwards.   Even if this be a dream, which
time is never destined to fulfil, its potency over men's

minds, while it endures, seems not diminished but augmented. It leavens all Western thought, and gives a shape to all Western policy. Administrative reforms were — administrative reforms. This was a social revelation.

The same illustrious person — it was Goethe — who wished that the Reformation had been conducted by men like Erasmus, rather than by a man like Luther, also deplored that the Revolution had hindered culture. Is not this to mistake the forces which stir and control men ? It would be well if political and social changes could be consummated with the same autumnal stillness and silence in which Nature works her transformations. But the ardent virtues, no less than the evil passions, of blind mortals, forbid this tranquil march through silent desolation to renovated life. Every mass of men in volcanic moments, like the mythic Etna, covers a Titan ; and it is by the Titan only that they can be moved. It is an evil, but not an unmixed evil, that this should be so. These violent rebellions against a spiritual or social destiny too hard to be longer endured, disclose heights of sacrifice and energy and aspiration in man, a tidal sweep and depth of moral force, which progress could ill afford to spare. We see the black gulfs, too, of human nature in such hours, but these are soon hidden, while the memorials of gigantic effort remain as a tide-mark for all time.

It is too commonly asserted, and straightway accepted, that the Revolution destroyed, but contributed nothing to the yet greater task of reconstruction; that it was wholly and unreservedly critical and negative; that we who have come after, vainly ransack the stores of its doctrines in search of instruments for the constructive enterprise imposed upon us, and find nothing but what is explosive, and calculated for desperate attack. Before adopting this as a final conviction, it is to be remembered that the same kind of accusation has been brought against the Reformation, and even against the moral doctrine of Christianity itself. The Christian ethics, it has been said, are too negative; they inculcate habitual self-denial, but are silent on the more urgent difficulties connected with the duties of self-assertion; they furnish no complete and positive scheme. The Reformation, again, is represented as no more than a critical movement; as if to transfer men's spiritual allegiance from the Church and tradition and the Papacy to the Bible, were not essentially an affirmative movement, and as if to bring into new and unexampled prominence such a doctrine—to take one instance of many—as that of election, pregnant as

it has shown itself in influence upon the lives and characters of those who accept it, could be described merely
as a removal of the props and shores of an old faith. For
one thing, merely destructive movements do not live.
They do not continue to give a light to one age of men
after another. The Revolution would not remain, as it
does in some shape or other, the main hope and faith
of so many of the most enlightened men on the continent of Europe, if it did not contain positive or
constructive elements. And looking, without prejudice,
at the proceedings from '89 down to the wretched
extinction of freedom at the hands of Napoleon, we
may detect under them all in the minds of the most
far-seeing actors, the fundamental elements of the
characteristically modern social growth.

/The Revolution, to begin with, impregnated the political atmosphere with ethical ingredients./ In other
words, details of government and public policy were
openly and practically declared to hang upon and to
be subordinate to moral conditions. Statecraft was
purged of its hypocritical forms, its unscrupulousness,
its pursuit of narrow and selfish ends through base
means, and the introduction of considerations of
morality as the paramount element in State affairs was
effected with a theoretic completeness that has been

constantly overclouded in practice, but has never been
shaken. If the mere cleansing of the old grooves of
policy was only negative, the translation of morality
from the formulas of the thinker into the dialect of
the chamber and the bureau, was a very distinctly
affirmative and positive process.

Since '89, Justice, as the radical condition of all
social arrangements, has taken up a place in the minds
alike of the politicians who evade it and of those who
conform to it, which neither Walpole, nor Frederick,
nor indeed any of the leading pre-revolutionary statesmen would have thought possible out of the closet
of a dreamer. The dogma of equality, itself in its
crudest form less barren in fruit of progress than it may
seem, led at once and directly to the establishment of
Justice as the pole-star of all social effort. Equality,
notoriously false if attributed to the actual condition of
men either at their birth or at any later time, is yet
full of meaning applied to the institutions of society ;
as society exists for the purpose of repairing the accidental inequalities of nature, and of giving to all the
same equality of external opportunity, The Revolutionists, fresh from Rousseau, mischievously treated
Nature as mild and beneficent, and society as harsh
and corrupting, when in truth a state of nature, un-

modified by all that we include in the agencies of society, would be the most deadly and degrading condition of life that we are able to conceive. But in spite of this intelligible confusion, they applied the conception of Justice, which they fancied they had borrowed from Nature—the cruellest and least righteous of all the immortals—to the organization and discipline of the State ; and hence its influence spread over the whole field of social life. The noble and elevating sense of public duty, the consciousness of deep moral obligation, of which Justice is the highest expression, almost forgotten as it had been, even in its narrowest form, amid the corruptions of Catholicism and the doctrinal disputatiousness of Protestantism, won a new, wider, and more enduring empire over the European mind.

Connected with this, and yet above this, sprang up the greatest of all the positive and constructive forces of the Revolution—the generous and sublime sentiment of the brotherhood of men. This was no new truth. It was at all events as old as Christianity, where it had begotten the sweet and holy precept of charity. But charity and brotherhood had fled from a Church that had invited the secular arm to dragonnades, not more nor less than from the Church which had drawn up and was administering the Penal Laws in Ireland. Paradoxical as it may sound, the tradition of love and charity which had been driven away from political Churches, found capacious shelter first in the profoundly humane spirit of Voltaire. The articles on Slavery, Punishments, and Persecutions in the *Philosophical Dictionary* are what the voice of the Church should have been, and had been, but was no more. It was Rousseau, however, who, filled with an ardent love for mankind, developed to the full the expansive forces of this divine sentiment, and proclaimed its sovereignty with a noble and touching eloquence that went straight to the heart of his generation.

The promulgation once more of this truth, not in a hortatory manner by theological doctors, but as the universal and heartfelt conviction of a nation, was the most splendid achievement of the Revolution, defaced as it was too soon afterwards by the extravagances of a panic for which the retrograde powers of Europe must be accounted mainly responsible. The sentiment of brotherhood was more than moral in France at this epoch. It was a religion, perhaps the highest, supported or not by a theistic apparatus, to which the human mind is capable of rising. The material misery and degradation of France in the eighteenth century kindled spiritual light in her, which fifty years of material prosperity and moral depravation have not altogether extinguished. Her own sufferings inspired an eager sympathy for all the rest of the family of men, and a high-minded zeal that they also should partake of the gifts which had been won by her efforts and sacrifice. The manner of all this has seemed to those of slower imagination to be theatrical : seen with more sympathetic eyes, it is bright with the glow of religion and humanity.

Consciously or unconsciously, the men of the generation immediately after '89 derived warmth and inspiration from this fervid outburst, and as a consequence of this special characteristic of it. Even those who opposed the Revolution caught a measure of brightness and largeness from their adversary. Followed as it was by reaction, yet the reactionists were reactionists of the highest pitch. De Maistre in philosophy, and Chateaubriand in religion, irresistibly penetrated with the positive elements of the very movement which they detested, were of a strangely different size and type from any predecessors they had in other times of reaction. The influence of Rousseau seems plainly perceptible in every page of the *Génie du Christianisme*. The difference in temper, and, we may add, in practical influence, between this renowned book and the controversial defences and apologies which teemed forth from the English press during the eighteenth century, is the measure of the enlargement of mind and sentiment that had taken place in the interval.   Far inferior in intellectual weight and acuteness, and without erudition, yet it is marked by a fineness of sympathy, and a strong sense of the spiritual interest of all sorts and conditions of men, which had been entirely absent from religious literature since the beginning of the century.   Christianity emerges once more as something else than a scheme to be proved or to be disproved.   The writings of De Maistre, again, cannot be called reactionary in the sense of advocating a return to medievalism, as the Middle Age had been understood.   His ideas and standards of the superiority of the social organization of this period over the ancient organizations to which the Revolutionists ignorantly dreamt of returning, are distinctly coloured by that conception of progress which it is one of the glories of his enemies to have permanently established.   He demonstrated the inadequacy of the Revolution, but in a spirit which has itself plenty of critical and revolutionary marks.

Partly, we may find a reason for this mental expan-

sion in the colossal and unparalleled size of the ruins
which the French Revolution made in the public
system of Europe, and which gave something of sublime even to the horror of the beholders.   But another
and deeper reason is discovered in the breadth of the
positive contributions that had been made to the cause
of progress, which is at bottom identical with that
cause of order which the best reactionists had at heart
—the /conception of politics as a special and very
exalted branch of morals / the constant presence and
supremacy of justice as a condition of social welfare ;
and the ennobling consciousness of a universal responsibility and obligation among nations for common aid
and succour, / of the duty incumbent upon each of
sharing the beneficent products of its own endeavour
with all.

The red and lurid fascination of the guillotine still
blinds men to the intrepid enthusiasm exhibited alike
by the leaders and the people, both in '89 and in the
ever vilified '93.   Let us notice two points.   First,
their absolute unfamiliarity with public life, with the
necessity therefore of temporising, of compromise, of
aiming not too high, of conciliating masses of opposing
interest, made them the more effective organs for an
enthusiasm entirely unconnected with, where it was

not directly antagonistic to, the whole of the standing system. It fitted them to found a religion and a church, if they had been blessed in other conditions. As by the Revolution we mean a movement of ideas, of faith, of types and patterns, so far it was an immense advantage to have its confessors unfettered and free to spread their gospel in its extreme ideal form, and mighty with all its native energy. Men thus got a full glimpse of a possible future, which was soon shut out again by the thick curtain of the smoke of battles, but which has lingered in their memories, and reappeared in their dreams.

Secondly, from its practical side the inexperience of the revolutionists and of the nation that trusted its destinies to them, led to disaster, but not entirely in the way that is vulgarly supposed. It ruined them, not by their incompetency to control their internal affairs or to construct a new system of popular government, but because it blinded them to the fact that France was only one member of the European federation, and though they could count upon her, they were sure to call down the fierce hostility of all the other unrevolutionized governments. They had a half instinct of this when they invited neighbouring nations to throw off the yoke. They forgot that in no other nation did the same conditions exist, as those which had made themselves what they were.

Another way in which their inexperience rendered them weak was by making them timorous even in their internal activity. This will appear monstrous to those to whom the Revolution only means the Reign of Terror. But looking more closely than this, we may perceive on every hand signs of that nervous apprehension which may seize the bravest man, treading an unknown path in the darkness of midnight. Because men were inexperienced, they were apprehensive and fearful ; and because they were fearful, they were cruel. It was inexperience, moreover, which made France stand in sombre silence and with bowed head before the guillotine, at the doors of the prisons in September, in the sight of noyades. The despotism of kings had taught them unbounded deference for the authority of the hour.[1] Their kings had not taught them that the exercise of authority in the cruel shedding of blood was an exceptional performance, demanding exceptional resistance. If they had had the experience which men get in free governments, they

[1] As De Tocqueville puts it, " La même cause qui avait fait tomber si aisément la monarchie, avait rendu tout possible après sa chute."— *Ancien Régime*, p. 305.

would have saved France from excesses which have
both stained her name, and practically kept her back
in the advance to a just liberty.

Publicists have been in the habit of talking of the
political inexperience of the French at the time of the
Revolution, as if they had been like negroes under their
princes on the Gold Coast ; as if long training under
free institutions were an indispensable condition of the
smallest legislative and constructive capacity.   That the
absence of free institutions and of the possibility of
public life weakens a nation and diminishes its self-
respect, is proved, I think, not only by abstract considerations of a more general character, but by the fact
that the French have never been so morally strong, have
never shown so much self-respect, as in the free interval between the despotism of the Bourbons and the
despotism of the Bonapartes.   It has not, however, been
taken into account that the moral enthusiasm of such
a moment as that from '89 to '93 strikes out a kind
of intellectual light, which may guide men not less
securely than the light which has been slowly kindling
in centuries of political experience. This would not
be the only case in history of unquenchable fervour
supplying light and order to what looked like chaos.
When men have so deep and pressing an interest in

order as the French nation then had, neither capacity on the part of the leaders to devise an adequate government, nor willingness on the part of the people to conform to the requisitions of such a government, is at all likely to be wanting. The urgent demands of the hour were sufficient in a people possessing the intellectual shiftiness, the quick penetration, the comprehensive grasp so characteristic, not only of the remarkable men whom France produced in such abundance in the hour of her crisis, but of the entire generation to guarantee the conditions of a political cosmos The prime condition of all, that a nation should know how to obey, was satisfied only too well, as was shown first by the general acquiescence in the worst measures of the Convention, and afterwards by the prompt allegiance which was paid to Napoleon, when it appeared, falsely enough, that his authority and genius, themselves reactionary in the highest degree, were necessary for the repulse of the reactionists outside. Looking from the temper of the people to the capacity of the men who came to the front of affairs, we may perceive that if the Constituent Assembly, though containing leaders of the finest character, failed to see the true nature of the movement which they aspired to lead ; if the Legislative lived miserably and perished

miserably, through the shortsightedness of its creators,
who had made the co-operation of a bitterly hostile
king essential to its success ; yet the Convention at
least, notwithstanding its exceptional orgies and follies,
realised the nature of the work to be done, and dis-
played full ability to do it. From this side, a nation
does not seem unfitted by political inexperience. Take
the redaction of the famous Civil Code, the glories of
which have been piratically appropriated for/the retrograde military usurper,/who destroyed the Revolution
in entering into the fruits of its labour. The Convention gave the committee of legislation three months
for the preparation of the code. In one month Cam-
bacéres placed it upon the table. Let us recall what
this code is, and then ask ourselves what feat political
experience has performed comparable with this in-
credibly swift and finished achievement.[1]

[1] " Rien au monde," M. Quinet justly says, " ne fait plus d'honneur
aux Français que d'avoir été capables de se donner froidement, impass-
siblement, leur Code civil au milieu du délire même de 1793. C'est ce
qui montre le mieux les énergies indomptables de cette race. Il n'est
aucun peuple qui ait fait paraître cette puissance de raison civile dans
l'extrême danger de mort, la tête sous le couteau. Je ne crois pas que
les Romains aient rien fait qui en approche. On parle encore de ce
champ qu'ils ont acheté pendant qu'il était occupé par Annibal.
Qu'est-ce que cela auprès de ce champ des lois civiles acquis et donné
au monde par les Français, pendant que le monde les occupait, et les
tenait presque sous ses pieds."— La Révolution, ii. 110.

These general remarks have proceeded to an inexcusable length ; but to speak of the Revolution baldly, without explaining the sense in which I use the term, and the spirit in which I understand the events included in it, would have been more inexcusable still. To talk about the Revolution is to talk by implication and allusion, of the whole course of European history, from its earliest beginning and in every one of its departments. And yet half the things that are said of it spring from one theory of life and progress, and apply to one aspect of that amazing event, while by most of those who listen they are received in some totally different sense, and applied to some quite other aspect. To avoid this as well as was possible, I have distantly indicated some of the estimates of the subject in which I do not concur. Let us turn to the great chief who led the forces of European reaction.

It must be pronounced an evil stroke of destiny, when Burke, whose whole soul was bound up in order, peace, and gently enlarged precedent, found himself face to face with this portentous man-devouring Sphinx. He, who could not endure that a few clergymen should be allowed to subscribe to the Bible instead of to the Articles, saw the ancient Church of Christendom prostrated, its possessions confiscated, its priests

proscribed, and Christianity itself officially superseded.
The economical reformer, who when his zeal was hottest
declined to discharge a tide-waiter or a scullion in the
royal kitchen, who had acquired the shadow of a
vested interest in his post, beheld two great orders
stripped of all their privileges and deprived of all
their lands, though the possession in each case had been
sanctified by the prescription of many centuries, and
by the express voice of the laws. He, who was full
of apprehension and anger at the proposal to take away
a member of Parliament from St. Michael's or Old
Sarum, had to look on while the most august monarchy
in Europe was deliberately overturned. The man who
dreaded fanatics, hated atheists, despised political theorizers, and was driven wild at the notion of applying
metaphysical rights and abstract doctrines to public
affairs, was confident that he saw a vast kingdom given
finally up to fanatics, atheists, and theorizers, who
talked of nothing but the rights of man, and made it
their chief aim to set as wide a gulf as ruin and bloodshed could make, between themselves and every incident or institution in their own history, or in that of
any other country. The statesman who had once declared, and habitually proved, his preference for peace
over even truth, who had all his life surrounded him-

self with a mental paradise of order and equilibrium and belief, in a sudden and single moment found himself confronted by the stupendous and awful spectre which three centuries of accumulated effort had at length raised in their supreme hour, and which was destined not to be laid for perhaps as many centuries to come.

Yet this unkindness of fate, embittering as it did the closing days of a noble life, was not an unalloyed misfortune for us. Burke at least rose to the height of the transactions which he abhorred and denounced. For may we not believe that the Reformation was fundamentally a progressive movement, bringing into new prominence ideas that it was not well for men to forget ; and yet at the same time agree that Bossuet took a wider, loftier, more profound view, of the nature of social development, of the conditions of a rightly ordered life, of the needs and possibilities of humanity, than did any of the Protestant doctors, great and valiant men as there were among them ? We may, in the same manner, while conceding and gratefully admiring the gigantic impetus which the Revolution imparted to European growth, in the points which I have too dimly and briefly tried to mark, still find in the writings of its arch-enemy a wiser, deeper,

broader, and more permanent view of the elements of
social stability, of its priceless value, of its power over
the happiness of men, than it was possible for his
adversaries, disinterested and lofty as many of them
were, to arrive at in the midst of the storm and con-
vulsions that enveloped them.

It requires no singular or extraordinary observation
to perceive that men may take the wrong side in such
a manner, and under the influence of such ideas, as to
produce a more impressive and elevating effect than
if they had taken the right side in any other manner.
To be in the right as measured by wise definition and
logical standard, is not all : it is necessary to be in
the right with humanity and breadth.   Is not the
next best thing to this, to be in the wrong with
humanity and breadth ? There is a manner, that is
to say, of espousing a wrong cause, which proves the
possession of far finer qualities and a far finer general
apprehension of human requirements, than we shall
find in any but one or two of the very best of those
who espouse the cause that for the time is right.   In
a moral aspect, the fineness of the material of which
a friend's character is made, is surely far more important to me, than the correctness of his intellectual
impressions.   In the large controversies of the world,

the tone in which a man speaks may be far more important than the precise justice of his appreciation of a set of current events. Tom Paine was specifically more correct in his judgment of the transactions of the time, than Burke was. Yet nobody, I believe, pretends that the *Age of Reason* contains as wise, instructive, and durably useful thoughts as the *Reflections*. Dr. Price's treatise on Civil Liberty offers many just considerations, yet the most ardent lover of freedom, if he be sufficiently removed from these still smouldering fires, will agree that Burke's conceptions of liberty were full of a grander and higher meaning than Dr. Price's.

Romilly mentioning to a friend that the *Reflections* have got into a fourteenth or some other edition, wonders whether Burke is not rather ashamed of his followers. As he was inflamed with a burning anxiety to get his ideas transferred into the action of a crusade, Burke was not likely to think much about the exact degree of the enlightenment of the people who bought his book and believed in it. Still he might have suspected himself, when he found that he had given deep pleasure to such a person as the King. The leader of a reactionary movement may sometimes, as in this case, claim a measure of admiration from us. It is when we come to the rank and file of reaction, the

s

greedy bishops, the fat-headed squires, the hide-bound politicians, the crass princes, that we find it hard to forgive the man of genius who made himself the organ of their selfishness, their timidity, and their blindness. We know that the parts of his writings on French affairs to which all these mean souls would fly, could not be the parts which men now read with delighted sympathy, but the scoldings, the screamings, the unworthy vituperation with which, especially in the latest of them, he attacked everybody who had a hand in the Revolution, from Condorcet and La Fayette down to Marat and Couthon. It was the feet of clay that they adored in their image, and not the head of fine gold and the breast and the arms of silver. They were grovelling in terror for their tithes and their rents, for their privileges and immunities in law-making and law-breaking, for their sinecures and pluralities, for a supremacy which they had seldom actively used except to originate a folly, or to perpetuate an oppression. Is there any spectacle more grievous in history than this of such a crew, led by such a man as Edmund Burke, and dragging after them such a man as William Pitt?

The ideas engendered of the attempt to subdue the American colonists, the pestilent reaction upon the national character of the crime of holding Ireland by

the bonds by which we then held it, the overflowing
of arbitrary and despotic notions from India—all these
we have already looked upon as preparatives for that
state of ignoble enslavement into which England fell
at this time, an enslavement to the imperious selfishness and shortsightedness of the ruling classes. But
in all these preliminary events, Burke had been the
eloquent and untiring enemy of the sections and the
opinions, to which he now lent the support as of an
oracle from the eternal gods. We may be sure that
the motives which were at the bottom of his envenomed
war against the Revolution, were different from the
motives of the men who chose him for leader. We
owe him this justice. He hated the tenor of affairs
in France with a large and understanding hatred. He
knew what it was that he was attacking, and he knew
distinctly both why he attacked it, and how his present
views were no more than the fair corollaries of the
views which he had maintained throughout a public
life of five and twenty years. His clamorous admirers
perceived little more than that the strongholds of privilege had gone down before the cry for liberty, like the
walls of Jericho before the voice of the trumpet, and
they were instantly filled with a blind and sinister
antipathy to every part of a movement which they

felt might eventually undermine the foundations of their own strongholds. What the Revolution meant, where its errors lay, why its aspirations were premature, to what high ends these aspirations pointed, were matters on which no power on earth could have enlightened them. They were simply the creatures of a blind and black hatred. Of Burke's writings, on the other hand, it may be truly said that the further we get away from the immediate passions of that time, the more surprisingly do we find how acute, and at the same time how broad and rational his insight was, though neither acute nor broad enough. I am not sure that they who most desire the consummation of the Revolution, will not also be those who find most to admire in his remarks upon this phase of it. Perhaps in the lapse of very many scores of years, when the ends which the French Revolution vainly pursued have been reached by a long process, of which it was the first stage, the *Reflections* will be accepted as furnishing, what is upon the whole, and in a large philosophic sense, the soundest contemporary criticism we possess.

This famous composition was written in 1790, the year of Federations, Feasts of Pikes, the steady growth of the Constitution under the hands of the Assembly, and the time when everything wore its happiest and most auspicious aspect. On Burke the apparently bright signs of the hour made no impression. They did not for a moment destroy his conviction, which subsequent events so signally confirmed, that the plan which the Constituent Assembly had followed was hopeless from its outset. He spoke of the virtuous and high-minded men who were conspicuous in that Assembly, in language of shamefully unjustifiable harshness. The contempt which he had for their scheme was more reasonable. At a moment when Robespierre himself fully believed that he was a royalist, and that a monarchic constitution would stand, Burke perceived that the memorable Sixth of October, when the King and Queen and the Assembly were conducted with triumphant violence from Versailles to Paris, was the virtual dethronement of Louis XVI., the final alienation of the monarch from the movement which had so outraged his authority, and the virtual transference of supreme power to the rabble of Paris. " Excuse me," he says, " if I have dwelt too long on the atrocious spectacle of the Sixth of October, 1789, or have given too much scope to the reflections which have arisen in my mind on occasion of the most important of all revolutions which may be dated from that day ; I mean a revolution in sentiments, manners, and moral opinions."[1]   It was precisely this revolution of sentiments and moral opinions, which might have taught the Constituents that their honourable toil was bootless.   Its sacro-sanctity had been stripped away in the minds of the people from the kingly office.   The King in person had received insults which he would have been more than mortal if he could have placidly forgotten, or loftily forgiven.   He had been brought up, let us remember, in a court where majesty was as powerful and holy as in Turkey; his consort was the daughter of a heroic Queen, whose heart had never for an instant fainted before accumulated troubles and wrongs, which surpassed even those of Marie Antoinette.   Yet this was the pair on whose sincere amity and cordial co-operation the Constituents counted for the success of their projects.

Another side of the acts of the Assembly presented itself to Burke in a way which subsequent events have shown to be perfectly just.   Their geometrical division of the country, their isolation of the different bodies, to say nothing of the confiscation of Church lands, and the entire change of administrative forms and agents, he compared to the treatment which a con-

Reflections, Works, i. 411, _a._

quered country receives at the hands of its conquerors. " The policy of such barbarous victors who contemn a subdued people and insult their feelings, has ever been, as much as in them lay, to destroy all vestiges of the ancient country, in religion, in policy, in laws, and in manners ; to confound all territorial limits ; to produce a general poverty ; to put up their properties to auction ; to crush their princes, nobles, and pontiffs ; to lay low everything which had lifted its head above the level, or which could serve to combine or rally in their distresses the disbanded people, under the standard of old opinion. They have made France free in the manner in which those sincere friends to the rights of mankind, the Romans, freed Greece, Macedon, and other nations. They destroyed the bonds of their union, under colour of providing for the independence of each of their cities." [1] Does this image involve any exaggeration either of the destruction of the old order that had taken place, or of the perilously equal surface which was left in its stead ? Mirabeau was the only Frenchman of the time who appears to have perceived this all-important fact, and the consequences that might be drawn from it. While Burke was taunting the Assembly with pursuing the levelling policy of con-

[1] *Reflections*, Works, i. 450, *a*.

querors, Mirabeau was secretly writing to the King
that their plan of reducing all citizens to a single
class would have delighted Richelieu. ⌠ " This equal
surface facilitates the exercise of power. Many reigns
in an absolute government would not have done as
much as this single year of revolution, for the royal
authority." ⌡ This, says De Tocqueville, was to understand the Revolution *en homme capable de la conduire.* [1] ⌡

Burke was guided to the very same exact appreciation of the Revolution as Mirabeau, not by the
instinct of a man with the capacity and resolution
to control it, but by sheer force of political genius,
which enabled him, in the least eventful year of the
whole movement, to discern that a mischief had been
done from which French liberty might never recover.
France, as he saw, was precisely in the condition of a
conquered country, though the master destined to avail
himself of the conquest had not yet come upon the
scene. Mirabeau hoped that he might in the name of
the King take possession of the dwelling that had been
thus swept and garnished. Fate had not decreed it so.
Napoleon grasped the sovereignty which Mirabeau had
aimed at. Burke could not foretell who the usurper
would be. What he foresaw was, that freedom at

[1] *Ancien Régime,* p. 11.

least was certainly impossible on that naked level. The first condition of freedom is, that men should have the power and habit of acting in united bodies on some commonly accepted principles, and with something like traditional methods. In 1790 every accepted principle, every traditional method had vanished, and the rigid and multiplex system of election had done everything to draw lines between bodies of men, instead of binding them together. " If the present project of a republic should fail," Burke said, with marvellous prescience, "all securities to a moderate freedom fail with it. All the indirect restraints which mitigate despotism are removed ; insomuch that, if monarchy should ever again obtain an entire ascendancy in France under this or any other dynasty, it will probably be, if not voluntarily tempered at setting out by the wise and virtuous counsels of the prince, the most completely arbitrary power that ever appeared on earth." To foresee the Empire in 1790 was a feat of sagacity to which probably no man in Europe except the writer was then competent.[1]

---

[1] *Reflections*, Works, i. 451. I do not know whether it was before or after this, that Napoleon first saw Corneille's *Cinna*, which acted upon him, he said, as a downright illumination ; ''et j'aperçus clairement dans la politique et dans la poésie des horizons que je n'avais pas

The Assembly, as we may now see clearly enough, were misled by a confused idea of that equality which had been placed in the front of revolutionary doctrine. The rightful equality of all men before the law became only one of many forms of a dogma, which, translated into other departments of political activity, is as mischievous as any idea that ever was invented. That the expediency of legal equality of rights should be connected with some false notion of the actual moral equality of men was bad enough, but that from all this there should be derived a firm faith in the propriety of geometric equality of departments, arithmetic equality of elected bodies, and the rest, was very hard for a politician like Burke to endure the thought or sight of. Passion for symmetry seems to have overruled every other consideration. It was at the root of the impatience with which the Constituents beheld any fragment of the old system, and it aggravated the nature and the extent of every fault that they committed. They overlooked the truth, of which Burke reminded them, that in government there is an excellence of

encore soupçonnés, mais que je reconnus faits pour moi." The vigorous lines in which Cinna, in the opening of the Second Act, dissuades Augustus from restoring liberty to the Romans, would naturally possess a suggestive brilliance in the eyes of a man resolved on taking away liberty from the French.

composition far superior to any excellence in simplicity.[1]
The Assembly were justly open to this criticism,
because, unlike the Convention, who realised the exigencies of the crisis more correctly and firmly, they
were honestly doing their best to construct a constitution after the English type, which is highly complex.

It was Burke's cardinal mistake, as it was theirs, to
believe that the change could have been effected on
this basis. He ignored the sincerely constitutional
character of their intentions, through anger at their
total misapprehension of the only means by which, as
he thought, their intentions could be carried out. We
who have the advantage of living more than seventy-
five years after these events, and also of tranquilly
meditating upon them without the thunder of falling
Bastilles in our ears, and the irruptions of frantic
female rabble into our chambers, may see how impossible, and even undesirable, an enterprise it was, to

---

[1] "The nature of man is intricate ; the objects of society are of
the greatest possible complexity ; and therefore no simple disposition
or direction of power can be suitable either to man's nature, or to the
quality of his affairs. When I hear the simplicity of contrivance
aimed at and boasted of in any new political constitutions, I am at
no loss to decide that the artificers are grossly ignorant of their trade
or totally negligent of their duty. The simple governments are fundamentally defective, to say the least of them."—*Reflections*, Works,
i. 404, *b*.

transplant the peculiar and exceptional growth of English history, to a country whose history from the fourteenth century downwards had been so entirely different. Burke is now seen to have been egregiously superficial when he declared the pre-revolutionary constitution of France to be formed upon principles similar to ours.[1] There was, it is true, a monarchy, an aristocracy, a commonalty, with local parliaments, and the possibility of States-General, resembling in some sort our double chamber. But apparent similarity of social divisions and political forms may easily disguise a radical diversity in the whole conditions of public order. To give a nation a king with powers limited to suggestion, a house of hereditary peers, a house of popular representatives, and a government by cabinet, is not necessarily to give them the English constitution. Underneath the political forms are the vast forces of national temperament, ancient usage, the previous course of the national history, the stage of development. To maintain that these are absolutely beyond the reach of modification of the most radical kind, is to share a very common and a very coarse error. But it is a still worse error to assume that such modification may be effected instantly, and at

---

[1] *Letter to a Member of the National Assembly*, Works, i. 488, b.

will, by the imposition of legislative forms from without. /No identity or analogy between the outsides of two systems of government is to be taken for a certain sign that the concealed internal forces are the same, or that the seat of substantial power is the same.

Nominally, the governments of France and England were both monarchies—the one limited, the other absolute. But we may not stop at this first difference between them. There were many others, and of as much moment. The English system, in spite of the fragments of prerogative which George III. had by disreputable shifts and devices contrived to resume, was essentially aristocratic and oligarchic. The nobles and landowners governed the country through partially popular forms. But the monarchy in England was still much stronger against the aristocracy, than the latter in France was against the king. The weaker element in our system was still not so weak as the corresponding element in France. Again, the traditions of the State Church since 1688 had been aristocratic, and not monarchic. In France they were entirely monarchic and anti-aristocratic. Witness the comparatively small ado with which the Clergy went over to the side of the Third Estate in the disputes between the orders on the first meeting of the States-

General.   In each country the main spiritual power
allied itself with that branch of the temporal power,
which had defeated the other branch, in the contest
that grew up after the decay of the feudal system.
But in England, where somehow there seems a natural
tendency to compensation and equilibrium, such as it
is, the power of the Church and its aristocratic coad-
jutors was encountered by a strong body of Protestant
Dissenters.   This kind of balance was wholly absent
in France.   It may be said that the freethinkers there
supplied the resistance to the Church, which in England
came from the Independents.   One might have thought
so, but for the assured fact that the freethinkers in
power treated religion with the most timorous respect.[1]
Camille Desmoulins expressed their general feeling,
in his peculiar way, when he said, " Les rois sont mûrs,
mais le bon dieu ne l'est pas encore." Within the Church
there was contention, it is true.   The Low Clergy looked
upon the High Clergy much as the Third Estate looked
upon the Nobles.   But this was a contest within their
own forum.

The existence of a balance of forces is the elemen-
tary condition of constitutionalism.   For this we
require the constant play within certain bounds of a

[1] Cf. M. Quinet's La Révolution, i. 124–184, ii. 132–178, &c.

number of forces, none of which is so much superior in weight or energy to any of the rest as to be absolutely neutralizing. In France, neither in the spiritual nor in the temporal order was any action of this kind possible. Each institution and company of men was either too strong or too weak. Each stood apart in an isolation, which was not less complete for not being of an avowedly and violently unfriendly character. We look in vain for any spot of common ground on which a constitutional struggle could have been carried on. The aristocracy were a caste, despising the *roturiers* and every other class. The court was still jealous of the aristocracy. Even within a year of his execution, Louis XVI. is said to have apprehended attempts on the royal power from this side. The Third Estate, untrained in habits of united action, hating the nobles, and not loving the clergy, could plainly only carry on one sort of contest with their political superiors—a war *à outrance*. The moment that they insisted on vote by heads instead of by orders—thus, as they were double the number of either of the two other orders, assuming the entire power—it was clear that previous institutions had finally incapacitated their minds for entertaining the barest constitutional idea. Where you had classes separated by sharp and impassable boundaries, where the habit and manner even of moderate and fair political or religious encounter was unknown, where none of the rival parties to the conflict agreed as to a single premiss or first principle on which measures might have been discussed, and where one order insisted, by their arrangements, on being supreme in every decision, what chance was there for any free and various play of tolerably equal forces ?

The French constitutionalists, allowing their sanguine and patriotic feelings to overcome their judgment and vision of what was possible, tried ardently to carry out the hopeless project which Burke reviled them for neglecting, simply because he could not perceive that the means to which they resorted, and which, as he knew, could never lead to the end which he and they both desired, were the best and only means they had. The monarchy was the only centre from which they could work, and this was implacably hostile, in the first place, and in the second incurably weak, from its complete and unparalleled isolation. They were wrong, not in their choice of means, but in mistaking an impracticable for a feasible project. In talking to them about the English Revolution of 1688, and holding it up for admiration, their monitor showed a strange misconception either of the French or of the English crisis. And we find that in the writings subsequent to the *Reflections*, he evinces a much truer appreciation of events by more frequent reference to our revolution of the seventeenth century. More than this, by the end of 1791, when he composed the / *Thoughts on French Affairs,* /he had penetrated still further into the essential character of the Revolution. Any notion of a reform to be effected ˙after the decorous pattern of 1688, so conspicuous in the first great manifesto, had wholly disappeared. The changes in France, he had then discovered, bore little resemblance or analogy to any of those which had been previously brought about in Europe. It is a revolution, he said, of doctrine and theoretic dogma. The Reformation was the last revolution of this sort which had happened in Europe ; and he immediately goes on to remark a point of striking resemblance between them. The effect of the Reformation was ʄ to introduce other interests into all countries than those which arose from their locality and natural circumstances." / In like manner, " they who will examine into the true character and genius of some late events, / must be satisfied that other sources of faction, combining parties among the inhabitants of different countries into one connexion, are opened, and that from these

T

sources are likely to arise effects full as important
as those which had formerly arisen from the jarring
interests of the religious sects."/ It is a species of
faction which "breaks the locality of public affections." [1]   At all events, he deserves credit for the
promptitude and the completeness with which he
awoke from the marvellous dream of a Whig France.
That he should have ever fallen into it is not a little
strange.   He declined with his usual wisdom to suggest
any positive plan for the National Assembly, for
reasons which, if we remember the vehement confidence with which he had taken upon himself to hold
them and their proceedings up to the scorn of Europe,
appear extremely remarkable.   " Permit me to say,"—
this, in the letter to a member of the National Assembly
—" that if I were as confident as I ought to be diffident
in my own loose general ideas, I never should venture
to broach them, if but at twenty leagues' distance from

[1] Works, i. 564-5.   De Tocqueville has unconsciously imitated
Burke's very phrases.   " Toutes les révolutions civiles et politiques ont
eu une patrie, et s'y sont enfermées.   La Révolution française . . . on
l'a vue rapprocher ou diviser les hommes en dépit des lois, des traditions, des caractères, de la langue, rendant parfois ennemis des compa-
triotes, et frères des étrangers ; *ou plutôt elle a formé au-dessus de
toutes les nationalités particulières, une patrie intellectuelle commune
dont les hommes de toutes les nations ont pu devenir citoyens.*"—Ancien
Régime, p. 15.

the centre of your affairs. I must see with my own
eyes ; I must in a manner touch with my own hands,
not only the fixed, but momentary circumstances,
before I could venture to suggest any political project
whatsoever. I must know the power and disposition
to accept, to execute, to persevere. I must see all the
aids and all the obstacles. I must see the means of
correcting the plan where correctives would be wanted.
I must see the things : I must see the men. Without a
concurrence and adaptation of these to the design, the
very best speculative projects might become not only
useless but mischievous. Plans must be made for men.
People at a distance must judge ill of men. They do
not always answer to their reputation when you
approach them. Nay, the perspective varies, and shows
them quite other than you thought them. At a distance, if we judge uncertainly of men, we must judge
worse of *opportunities*, which continually vary their
shapes and colours, and pass away like clouds." [1] The
admiration which rises to our lips at these words is
stifled as soon as born, when we recall the confident,
unsparing, immoderate criticism which both preceded
and followed this most rational exposition of the danger
of advising, where we know neither the men nor the

[1] Works, i. 487, b.

T 2

opportunities. Surely unfaltering denunciation under
these circumstances was not much more befitting than,
as he admits, crude prescriptions would have been.

In suggesting, however distantly, the English scheme
of government on a monarchic basis as the remedy for
the disorders and misfortunes of France, Burke forgot
his own favourite doctrine of the relativity of all political systems, quite as fully as his adversaries did, and
perhaps a little less justifiably, when they returned to
the retrograde types of ancient organization. Talk
about Lord Somers was as much out of place on the
one side, as talk about Brutus and Gracchus or Lycurgus
and Solon on the other. It is to be said that his ideas
had the experience of England to a certain extent in
their favour, while the absolute rights of man which
formed so much of the stock of the revolutionists were
presented in the crudest shape, and assuredly received
little colour of experience from the way in which
they had been held or acted upon by the Greeks and
Romans. With all that he said against the intellectual
method of the Revolution, none will sympathise more
heartily than those who admire most both its general
aims and many characteristics of its moral spirit. The
rights of man would have furnished a scanty and
inadequate basis for the constitution of that state

which first brought them into practical politics, if
there had not been men endowed with the knowledge
which Hamilton and Madison had experimentally of the
principles of government. The Americans had all the
benefits of the rights of man, but then they had publicists who could construe and embody them in a
practical system. The wise and prudent temper which
found expression in the pages of the *Federalist*, unfortunately had no chance in the revolutionary hurricane.
The nearest approach which the French had to the
Federalist was in Sieyes, and we know how remote that
was. A man who could build constitutions out of his
own head by the dozen, naturally came to the front at a
time when a nation inspired with a violent hatred of
its own history was resolved to be indebted to the
teaching of experience for nothing, and to deduce all
its maxims of public action from a small set of *à priori*
principles, or a small collection of political and moral
ideals.

It has been already suggested in what way this
may have been useful to mankind, by bringing these
ideals into a bright and impressive prominence. But
nobody can help seeing how much deadly injury was
inflicted on the French people by this resolute adherence to deductive geometric methods. By adopting

a metaphysical standard, instead of one adjusted by the combination of general ideas with maxims derived more immediately from observation and experience, they were sure to erect an impracticable scheme, while they were at the same time and by the same process inflaming their own expectations by exaggerated and impossible hopes. The rights of men in government, as had been said, are their advantages.[1] The latter could never be reached by the most ardent scrutiny into the ultimate nature of the former. To construct an abstract entity, and then to evolve from its supposed properties practical laws, must always constitute a sterile, and if carried into operation on a great scale, a ruinous process. Incomparable in fecundity of material resources, in intellectual dexterity and promptitude, and in noble energy in the face of foreign interference, yet can anything be more barren in realised moral products than the French Revolution? Animated as the revolutionists were by some of the most powerful convictions that can enter into the human breast, by a belief in progress, in justice, in brotherhood, yet they seem to have been paralysed whenever they essayed any great incorporation of their ideas in positive institutions, or even in exten-

[1] Cf. ante, p. 31, and pp. 20–24.

sive measures of destruction, that required courage and faith.

Is not the key to this to be found in their method? Reasoning down from unsubstantial, unsupported conceptions, into which no single objective ingredient has entered from their origin down to the hour of their attempted realization, is the most chilling and fatal of enterprises, where large masses of men are to be dealt with. A sense of isolation ensues that is black and overwhelming to the spirit of man. The air that the philosopher may find full of warmth and peopled with the fanciful creations of abstract research, is to the mass a comfortless and appalling void. The soul cannot live and move in it. Cut off the experience of the race from him, and man trembles. The burning visions of a future of brotherhood, the most gracious side of the Revolution that is open to our contemplation, were inadequate without the support of a religious consciousness of what we owe to past effort. Not nourished by this, the other grew cold and grey. Those who detest the past with indiscriminate execration are sure, in the long run, to come to distrust the future also. The nation or the individual to whom the effort and experience of the race in all bygone time has become as a blank page, a mere doleful chronicle of blindness and wrong that has done nothing for us and contains no lesson for us, is the certain prey of a crushing reaction.

Alive to these impressions, we can imagine the sympathy with which, not merely vulgar-souled princes and divines, but less ignoble natures, vibrated to some of the admirable truths of the *Reflections.* "We are afraid," says the author in one place, " to put men to live and trade each on his own private stock of reason, because we suspect that this stock in each man is small, and that the individuals would do better to avail themselves of the general bank and capital of nations and of ages. Many of our men of speculation, instead of exploding general prejudices, employ their sagacity to discover the latent wisdom which prevails in them. If they find what they seek, and they seldom fail, they think it more wise to continue the prejudice with the reason involved, than to cast away the coat of prejudice, and to have nothing but the naked reason : because prejudice with its reason has a motive to give action to that reason, and an affection which will give it permanence. Prejudice is of ready application in the emergency ; it previously engages the mind in a steady course of wisdom and virtue, and does not leave the man hesitating in the moment of decision, sceptical, puzzled, and unresolved. Prejudice renders a man's virtue his habit, and not a series of unconnected acts. Through just prejudice, his duty becomes a part of his nature."[1] Is not this to say, in other words, that in every man the substantial foundations of action consist of the accumulated layers which various generations of ancestors have placed for him; that the greater part of our sentiments act most effectively when they act most mechanically, and by the methods of an established, unquestioned system; that although no rule of conduct or spring of action ought to endure which does not repose in sound reason, yet this naked reason is in itself a less effective means of influencing action, than when it exists as one part of a fabric of ancient and endeared association? This is a truth of human nature which even in time of revolution it is a monstrous fault to overlook. It certainly was not forgotten at the Reformation, which left a thousand undisturbed convictions and habits for each one that it destroyed or directly modified; nor in the English Revolution, when Cromwell manifested in every way his strong sense of the urgent necessity of forbearing to erase existing laws and to violate dominant ideas.

It was something very different from an inflam-

[1] Works, i. 414, a.

matory appeal to mere conservative passion, to bid
France beware of sundering the sacred links which
bind together the generations of men, and of rudely
cutting off the solemn perpetuity of the common-
wealth. It was to place the *Reflections* a long way
above the level of a heated pamphlet, to remind a
nation that there is a collective reason of ages, from
which they might not refuse to draw with impunity ;
that there is a continuity in affairs, without which
" men would become little better than the flies of a
summer." This may be Toryism, but it is Toryism on
its noble and exalted side.

The inauspicious pursuit of practical ends by abstract
modes was the natural consequence of the predominance of men of letters. All recent thought upon the
Revolution, the product of the most diversely trained
minds, coincides in fixing upon this circumstance a very
important share of the conditions which made the
movement a gigantic and terrible, if only transient,
failure. De Tocqueville's chapter on the causes which
made literary men the principal persons in France,
and the effect which this had upon the Revolution,
is only a little too cold to be able to pass for Burke's
own. Without the passion of a contemporary, he
dwells on the fatal characteristic of the writers of the

eighteenth century, and hence of the politicians who
drew their whole untempered inspiration from these
writers; how without exception they all believed that
the proper method is to substitute simple and elemen-
tary rules, drawn from reason and natural law, for the
complicated and traditional customs which regulated
the society of their time.[1]   M. Quinet's work is a
sermon, full of eloquence and cogency, upon the incapacity and blindness of the men who undertook
the conduct of a tremendous crisis upon mere literary
methods, without the moral courage to obey the logic
of their beliefs, with the student's ignorance of the
eager passion and rapid imagination of multitudes
of men, with the pedant's misappreciation of a people,
of whom it has been said by one of themselves, that
there never was a nation more led by its sensations,
and less by its principles.   Comte, again, one of whose
most special doctrines is that of the separation of the
spiritual and temporal powers, points impressively to
the Revolution as the period which illustrates more
decisively than another, the peril of confounding the
two great functions of speculation and political action.
He speaks with just reprobation of the preposterous
idea in the philosophic politicians of the epoch, that

[1] *Ancien Régime*, book iii. c. 1.

society was at their disposal, independent of its past development, devoid of any inherent impulse, capable of being morally regenerated by the mere modification of legislative rules.[1]

Nothing exhibits Burke's profundity of observation in contemporary matters more conclusively, than the promptitude and assurance with which he detected and held fast the fatal element, that all subsequent thinkers concur in declaring to have been the secret of the wreck.　Later writers have illustrated the operation of this element with greater elaboration, and explained the *rationale* of it with somewhat more of philosophic precision.　No one has illuminated it with a more penetrating and diffusive light.　Probably he did not see that the type of the relations proper for the philosopher in regard to political action, was embodied before his eyes.　Adam Smith, one of the most distinguished positive thinkers in this negative century, developed his opinions in serene and salutary tranquillity, undisturbed by the harassing necessity of modifying them so as to meet particular practical exigencies.　Then Pitt, who had assimilated them with masterly comprehension, proceeded to apply them in limited and modified forms to the solution of actual

---

[1] *Positive Philosophy*, vol. ii. book vi. c. 12 (Eng. Trans.).

problems. That this is the normal character of the influence of speculative minds upon public affairs, was shown by the success of Pitt's schemes, so long as he was permitted to carry them on without interruption. Is there, on the other hand, any satisfactory example of great political advantages being secured by the direct contact of minds, long habituated to abstract ways of surveying things, with the things themselves, which are mainly known to them through this diffracting medium?

What Burke did not see was, that a total change in the spirit of government was imperatively demanded, in order that the practical man might have space and power in which to carry out in a just and prudent manner the projects of the wise thinker. The Revolution is a movement of which the object and effect is to widen this space and augment this power. The gulf between the conclusions of the intellect, and existing institutions and methods of statesmanship, had become too broad and deep to be endurable. In France, especially, the kingdom had been brought to the very brink· of ruin long before '89. The antagonism between old forms and the new spirit, with the violent wreck that came of it, was essentially the work, not of the Revolution, but of the monarchy.

In England, as Pitt was in one part of his career
the type and example of a judicious statesman, open
to ideas, yet not frantically possessed by them, so in
another part he made plain the incompatibility between
the demands of the new time, and the maintenance of
the forms of the old.   Burke might have admitted that
some such event as the French Revolution was necessary to emancipate the statesman, if he had lived to
see all the consequences, as we see them, of the refusal
of George III. for example, to accede to Pitt's views on
the Catholic question.   He would have thought the
unjust government of an important member of the
empire, the maintenance of a grievous sore in the
national administration, destined for tens of years to
spread and rankle, draining us of material strength,
and covering us with moral shame — all this,
which has come of the King's conduct in 1801, he
would surely have thought too dear a price to pay
for the privilege of maintaining a perpetuity of hollow
forms, which only stifled the freedom and progress of
all the objects for which they had ever existed.

He believed that the transactions in France meant
the rule of theorists and " the methodising of anarchy."
Assuredly, if it had meant the first, it would have
meant the second also.   But nobody now doubts that

to uphold lifeless and rotten forms is a still more effectual and dangerous means of methodising anarchy than even this. To give power in the temporal order to blind princes, or a narrow and selfish class, and in the spiritual order, to endow with wealth and dignity and the privilege of teaching a nation, bodies of men, all from their traditions and formulas far below the highest moral and intellectual level of their time, while in thus doing you are crippling the able and beneficent, and discouraging high and honest thought— this was, and remains, the really anarchic process. A cabinet of dreamers at the head of an empire may be a dreadful spectacle, portending woe and shipwreck. But a system which—as the old régime did, and as its remnants still do—rears a tremendous barrier between the ideas of the thinker and the possibility of their fulfilment, which prevents political action from keeping pace in some sort with the best political speculation, and which gives spiritual prerogatives to men who are lowest in spiritual worth, is infinitely more portentous and unsound.

Fatally deficient as the Revolution was in positive principles, yet as time cools our passion and gives us a juster perspective, this will become more and more clear, that the apparent lawlessness and confusion of the last ten years of the century were less, not greater, than the lawlessness and confusion which had been universal since the Regency. The Terror itself, which has occupied a space in men's minds so entirely out of proportion alike with its actual destructiveness and its latent political significance, was leniency and order compared with the methods by which Christianity had propagated itself in the hands of the Inquisition, of Alva, of the English Protestants in Ireland, of the dragoons of Louis XIV. Men have vented bitter sarcasms on the dissemination of Liberty and Fraternity by the guillotine, and have laughed at the missionary cry of "*Sois mon frère, ou je te tue.*" Would it be so much less difficult for some Burke of the other side, to paint Religion stalking over Europe with words of charity and blessing and brotherly love on her lips, with the cord and the knife and the torch in her hands, with her feet crimson and wet with the blood of slaughtered confessors? Once more, let us be just. Crimes, as Burke has taught us, are the acts of individuals, and not of denominations of men. The Revolution had fierce and anarchic sons, but then it found ferocity and anarchy.

That order in Church and State which Burke deplored the loss of, was a mere thin semblance of order.

Dazzled by the whiteness of the sepulchre, he refused to see that, inside, it was full of dead men's bones and corruption. Compared with that benign and holy Church which he figured in his sensitive and sympathetic imagination, the reign of Fouquier Tinville, of Hébert, of Collot d'Herbois, of Couthon, was monstrous and unendurable enough. But the benignity was imaginary. If the Revolution had its *suspects* and its *suspects d'être suspects,* so had the Church. In the middle of the eighteenth century to be suspected of cognisance of a Calvinistic assembly, of which they had not given notice to the authorities, even though they had taken no share in the proceedings, was punishable in the case of a woman by imprisonment, and in the case of a man by the galleys of Toulon. A house which was believed to have given shelter to a Calvinist pastor was razed to the ground even so late as 1754.[1] All offences in matters of religion were punished, in the words of a royal ordinance, *sans*

---

[1] M. Chassin's *Génie de la Révolution,* ii. 161. Whether we like or dislike M. Chassin's theory of the Revolution, everybody will be grateful for the industry which has ransacked the Cahiers of 1789, the pamphlets and the *procès-verbaux,* and by copious and accurate transcription, has presented us with a photographic reproduction of the grievances and aspirations of the hour, which to the foreign student at least is invaluable. The work unfortunately is still unfinished.

forme ni figure de procès." If two newly-converted
persons ventured to get married out of France, their
parents, guardians, and tutors were supposed to deserve
the galleys, banishment, and confiscation. To have a
marriage sanctified by the blessing of a Calvinist pastor
was to be guilty of relapse ; the husband went to the
galleys, the wife to prison, for life. To be married
except by a priest and unless according to Catholic
usage was to live in concubinage, to have a dishonoured
wife and to produce bastards. I recall all this, not to
show that Catholics in France were as severe to a
minority in France, as the Protestants were to the
majority in Ireland, but to point out its results in a
political sense. It is calculated by different authorities
that there were in the last part of the old régime
between four and five hundred thousand of these
Calvinistic and illegal unions. There was thus about
a twentieth part of the population, and not the least
virtuous part of it, living in concubinage. There were
three or four generations of bastards, and the consequent disturbance of inheritances overwhelmed everything in a confusion that at last became intolerable.[1]

In 1787 appeared the Edict, which conceded a
measure of civil rights to the non-Catholics. They

[1] Chassin, ii. 167.

might be born, married, and buried without a false
and hypocritical recognition of the religion of the
State. They might follow any calling except that of
a teacher or a judge. They were henceforth admitted
to all the advantages and rights of property and suc-
cession. But the free exercise of their religion was
as little permitted as ever. Whoever should allow
himself to speak against the State religion would be
punished with all rigour. They were bound to contribute to the maintenance of the State religion ; they
were still forbidden to presume to look upon themselves as a body or corporation, or to perform the
slightest act in any collective capacity. It is clear,
therefore, that the Church had no right to complain.
The only thing that the Edict did was to give a civil
status to the Calvinists and other non-Catholics. Yet,
mark the spirit in which that vast body whom Burke
viewed as the guardians of truth and the bulwarks of
order, received this attempt to stay a mortal civil
confusion. Solemn remonstrances poured in upon the
King from every side. The release of women from
the prisons, the return of men from the galleys, the
registration of clandestine marriages, the legitimation
of children, made the clergy cry out in holy anguish,
"Ah ! Sire, quelle source inépuisable d'amertumes pour

l'Église, et de séductions pour les enfants, si l'indulgence de la nouvelle législation préparait la voie à un
tolérantisme universel ?" [1]　　Another Assembly prayed
the King to leave this evil path, and to complete the
noble task that Louis the Great began and Louis the
Well-Beloved had continued. The new France, when
its hour arrived, did not forget this.

"Who but a tyrant," cried Burke, who did forget it,
"could think of seizing on the property of men, unac-
cused, unheard, untried, by whole descriptions, by
hundreds and thousands together? Who that had
not lost every trace of humanity could think of
casting down men of exalted rank and sacred function, some of them of an age to call at once for
reverence and compassion, of casting them down from
the highest situation in the commonwealth, wherein
they were maintained by their own landed property,
to a state of indigence, depression, and contempt?"
The spectacle was sad, but the champion of these
venerable sufferers might have remembered that they
too had seized on the property, and destroyed the
freedom and happiness, of whole descriptions of men,
unheard and untried. Surely, their exalted rank and
sacred function rather aggravated than palliated the

[1] Chassin, ii. 178.

incorrigible and envenomed animosity with which they had hunted down men and women whose only sin was the disbelief of a portion of their creed. No curse fell upon them, which they were not at that last moment eager to inflict upon unoffending Calvinists. "When not possessed of power," asked their defender, "were they filled with the vices of those who envy it ? Goaded on with the ambition of intellectual sovereignty, were they ready to fly in the face of all magistracy, to fire churches, to massacre the priests of other descriptions, and to make their way over the ruins of subverted governments to an empire of doctrine, sometimes flattering, sometimes forcing the consciences of men from the jurisdiction of public institutions into a submission to their personal authority, beginning with a claim of liberty and ending with an abuse of power ?" Divesting this of its rhetorical turn of phrase, and considering the attitude and voice of the clergy, both high and low, in reference to the Edict of 1787, we may answer the question thus put in the triumphant expectation of a negative, with a very decisive affirmative.

The men who, in the last year of the old epoch, could speak of toleration as the climax of evil and bitterness, proved that it was they who maintained anarchy, and that the men who drove them from their seats were performing a process indispensable for the restoration of a lasting order. The modern inquirer who reflects on these events, will be disposed only to complain that the Revolution treated its spiritual enemy with but too little resolution. It was not by such forbearance and fostering as the Convention extended to Catholicism, that Catholicism vanquished Paganism, or that the Reformers vanquished Catholicism. "The French Revolution," said De Maistre, "was commenced against Catholicism, and for democracy : the result will be for Catholicism against democracy." It may end so for our time. If it does, this will be partly due to the reluctance of democracy to falsify its own principles by resorting to the ignoble but effective weapons employed by its desperate foe.

In the secular order we find equally that there could be no worse blunder than to impute anarchy to the movement which only made it visible, but was innocent of all share in its origin. The thin decorous veil of a settled administration, with divisions of function and just varieties of rank and place, sufficed to hide from Burke, and from many who have thought and written since his time, the profound disorder, confusion, and wrong which ravaged France behind the veil. If we think upon *lettres-de-cachet*, upon the system of secret police and of secret procedure, upon the exceptional tribunals, upon the vexatious and tyrannical interference of military and fiscal officers with the private liberty of the citizen, upon the forced services of various kinds—in a word, upon all the grievances which figure so monotonously and so grievously in the documents of '89, and if we realise what they all mean, we shall admit that the sin of anarchy lies, not at the door of those who could endure it no longer, and rose up with flaming eyes and laid resolute hands upon it, but with those others who had first created this evil and tempestuous chaos. To interfere with the property of a large order collectively, is no worse than habitual interference with the property of individuals taken singly. If the revolutionists did the first, not less certainly the king, nobles, and clergy had done the second. If the confiscation of the Church lands was anarchic, when its proceeds went to the purposes of the nation, what can we say of the petty but prolonged private confiscation of the possessions of individuals, when its proceeds went to foster the pride of the nobles, and to support the monstrous extravagances of the court? The revolutionists did not plunder the Church and the nobles for themselves. They did not turn to the faith of the Revolution as the English aristocracy turned to the faith of the Reformation, to glut themselves on abbey lands, and batten on the proceeds of a selfish spoliation. Marat was found by Charlotte Corday in a squalid garret, with elevenpence halfpenny in ready money. Saint Just fed, like a Spartan, on black-broth. Robespierre lodged humbly with a cabinet-maker. And it was the same with the rest. None of them gained anything, except the few that by and by took service under the man who came up and scotched the Revolution, and plundered its goods. The revolutionists did not despoil the people in the name of the people, as others have done since, nor in the name of the king, as had been done before, for the private gain of the spoilers. Whatever was taken went to the common stock.

The body of the people, according to Burke, and very truly so far, must respect the property of which they cannot partake. ["They must labour," he continues, "to obtain what by labour can be obtained; and when they find, as they commonly do, the success disproportioned to the endeavour, they must be taught their consolation in the final proportions of eternal justice."] This was the way in which the great proletarian tragedy presented itself to him. Unmistakably he was here falling into slavery to those metaphysical abstractions from which in every other part he keeps so free. What was eternal justice to eighteen millions of creatures, perishing of hunger ? A Lyons silk-weaver, working as hard as he could for over seventeen hours a day, could not earn money enough to procure the most urgent and bare necessaries of subsistence. With what benignity of brow must Eternal Justice have presented herself in the garret of that hapless wretch. The Lyons electors in '89 showed this in their documents. If, they argued, we only look upon the silk-weavers as mechanical instruments requisite for the manufacture of stuffs, if one only treated them as domestic animals kept for the sake of their labour, even then it would be necessary to furnish them with such means of living as we give to the domestic animals.[1]

Again, are we to be so overwhelmed with sorrow over the pitiful destiny of the men of exalted rank and sacred function, as to have no tears for the forty thousand serfs on the slopes and in the gorges of the Jura, who were held in dead-hand by the Bishop and chapter of Saint-Claude ? /" Enfin," they closed the exposition of their woes, " enfin c'est justice que nous

[1] Chassin, i. 181-205.

demandons."[1]/ Their ideas of eternal justice were
something more than an idle abstraction, sounding
forth from pulpits or across the pages of the champions
of order. It was no metaphysical right of man for
which they cried with such simplicity and moderation,
but only the practical right of being permitted to save
themselves by their own toil from cold, and hunger,
and the degradation of the beasts. Of these *main-
mortable* serfs of ecclesiastics, there are variously said
to have been a million, and a million and a half, at
the time of the Revolution. Our horror, as we think
of the priests and prelates who left palaces and dignities
to earn a scanty living by the drudgery of teaching
languages in strange lands, is sensibly alleviated by the
thought that a million or more of men were rescued
from a ghastly material misery, and the mental bondage
which attended it. The picture of the Bishop of Saint-
Claude in mean circumstances becomes very support-
able, when it is presented as an essential condition of
the restoration to humanity of his forty thousand serfs.
The vision of the final proportions of eternal justice
perhaps grows a little brighter in one's eyes, at the
thought.

[1] Chassin, i. 159–161. M. Chassin promises an *in extenso* transcript
of this document in his third volume.

We have already seen how in Indian affairs Burke's sympathy with the oppressed millions was undisturbed by his imaginative sympathy with august princes and powerful ministers. In the more momentous and overwhelming affairs of France, we cannot say the same. Admire as we may, and as we ought, his hostile and reasoned judgment against the revolutionary methods, his extraordinary foresight into some of their remote consequences, his general theory of the sacredness of order; still, at the bottom of all, we discern that the lessons deducible from all European history, that of England not excepted, had not yet made themselves felt within his mind. He shows no consciousness that feudalism and Catholicism, in a certain stage of progress the most binding and indispensable of social conditions, had now, in their season of decay, grown bitterly and fiercely anti-social. Instead of uniting men, and cementing different interests, by strong and common beliefs in the spiritual order, and in the temporal order by protecting the germs of industrial development, the nobles and the clergy had each fallen into a state that was incompatible with the maintenance of any further semblance of social union. When men spoke of France, what did they mean ? A compact society, striving by

different instruments and in various ways, for the
promotion of some set of common national aims—such
a society as we may now see very partially realized
in America, in England, or in Germany? Alas! what
they meant was very far removed from this. France,
instead of being one society, was in truth an emphatically anarchic accretion of heterogeneous, hostile, and
irreconcilable interior societies. To which of these
can we point as being penetrated by the sincerely
social feeling? Not the clergy; they were prepared
to wreck the state, rather than suffer any derogation
of the special dignities and privileges of their Church.
Not the nobles; at the first or second alarm, with a
precipitancy that stamps them as the most ignoble of
men, deficient even in the solitary virtue of aristocracy,
they fled to beat up foreign enemies against their own
countrymen, as the Greek and Italian oligarchs used
to do. Not the King and Queen; fed and nurtured,
as they were, upon a haughty, absolutist, and now
baneful tradition.

It is the essence and significance of all separate
classes—capitalist, hereditary, aristocratic, monarchic—
to be more or less anti-social in the modern stage,
until they have learnt by patient, disinterested, and
humane meditation that the claims of the multitude

are sovereign and paramount, just because it is the multitude. In it you have the only body whose real interests can never, like those of minor classes and special orders, possibly become anti-social. Burke had, as we have seen, fully understood and accepted this truth, and to have done so was one of his most remarkable titles to recollection and distinction in the chronicles of the English constitution. Nothing but his almost uncontrollable passion for anything which only so much as looked like order, could have blinded him to the fact that even the best of classes and divisions have a strong natural tendency to become anti-social, or to the other fact that the classes and divisions then standing in France, so far from being the best, were probably the most sinister, the most fatally committed to anti-social courses, that the civilized world has ever seen. A quarter of a century before the Revolution, he had proclaimed that a law against the majority of the people is in substance a law against the people itself; its extent determines its validity."[1] It would be interesting to know what the royal exiles and patrician emigrants, his friends of later years, would have thought of such a doctrine as this —they, who had habitually and deliberately looked

[1] *Tracts on the Popery Laws,* Works, ii. 436, b.

upon their own narrow order as constituting in substance the people and state of France. Their delusion
was natural. The whole fabric of their institutions
stood, an arsenal of cunning engines for the moral
depression and material ruin of the majority. The
meaning of the Revolution was the emphatic declaration over Europe that the majority of the people *are*
the people.[1]

This lay at the bottom of the cries for liberty, which
our generation is apt to find a little empty and unmean-
ing. The partisans, both of old absolutism, and of its
modern sequel, democratic despotism, ask, as Burke
did, What is liberty without wisdom and without
virtue? and they reply to themselves, as he did, that
"it is the greatest of all possible evils, for it is folly,
vice, and madness, without tuition or restraint." The
orators of the Revolution, thinkers of a later period,
and some persons interested in finding arguments for
Bourbonism at one time, and Bonapartism at another,
have all combined to show how difficult it is to talk
of freedom, without falling either into an egregious
common-place, or an egregious sophism. To declaim, as
Dr. Price does, about liberty being the foundation of all

---

[1] Cf. Chassin, i. 279, where the reader may see the strong way in
which an anonymous pamphleteer of '89 put this.

honour, and the chief privilege and glory of our natures, is a rather misleading commonplace. To answer, as Mademoiselle de Launay did, a question as to the seat of the most perfect liberty, that it was the Bastille, is a very mischievous sophism. The Revolutionists, or some of them, inclined to the first. Burke inclined, more distantly, to the second. The one exaggerated its positive influence and power: the other looked too exclusively to the mischiefs of folly or madness left unrestrained. The one worshipped political liberty as the single fountain of moral liberty : the other postulated a wide and perfect condition of moral freedom as the indispensable preliminary of fitness for political freedom.

It would be unpardonable if anybody who had studied the writings of Burke should forget that we ought to look at all this relatively, and not absolutely. A disciple of Rousseau might have maintained, that in every stage of the development of the race, every individual is the better for possessing unfettered liberty to do as he will. There is no modern thinker, however, who does not believe that in the rudimentary phases of social life, this would not only be a misfortune, but an impossibility. The continuance of social life upon such terms would be hopeless. To give to an infant the rights and liberties of the adult, is doing much to prevent it from ever becoming an adult. Early communities rise to the rank of societies by forcible deprivation of liberty, or, may we not say, by reason of their ignorance of what liberty means. To call upon a tribe, bare of organization, and untrained in orderly function, to govern themselves by popular forms, is to invite dissolution and instant retrogression. So far as a barbarous, tribal element of this sort remains in a civilized society, so far it needs the concentration of the government; not because the governing body or individual is likely to be very far above the average of the subjects, in knowledge, judgment, or any other of the great political qualities, but simply because concentration is an indispensable condition of advance from the tribal state, or even of existence in it.

One would suppose, from the tone adopted by Burke, and other more decided and systematic champions of oligarchic and strong monarchic governments, that the revolutionary question was between the possession of sovereignty by a very wise body, and its possession by a very fatuous crowd. In practice, this kind of gulf is not found. If the majority of the people,—that is, if the people,—are ignorant and narrow, it is certain

that any set of men who successively and normally
rule over them, will also partake of this ignorance and
narrowness. We cannot have a wiser or nobler
government than the average social state of the time
allows. On the other hand, a nation having grown in
wisdom and skill, while its rulers have stood still,
may awake to find itself governed by men infinitely
below its own average. This was the state in which
France found herself in '89, and she was instantly
sensible that this, if anything could be, was a state of
slavery and bondage. Her cry for liberty was no mere
sentimental shriek for an abstraction, whose realization would have been the ruin of the nation. Translated into other words, it was simply a demand that
the government of the country should raise itself to
that height of moral liberty which the average masses
were conscious of having reached. Political liberty
is, under all circumstances, the only possible guarantee
that the principles, and methods, and purposes of
a national government shall not sink below this
moral level of the nation itself. It corrects the
tendencies of a government in that direction by mild,
but effective and prompt means, by securing a steady
and constant pressure upon the Cabinet, the Chamber,
or the President. Where there is not this political

x

liberty, this recognised right and method of directly and habitually infusing the opinions of the majority into the governing organ, whatever it may be, there is only one remedy when the difference between the two grows irreconcilable, and that is, the destructive and perilous remedy of a violent revolution.   If we reflect that the history of every civilized and social state that has existed within the range of our chronicles, proves that no government in the world has gone on for three generations without demanding modification at the hands of the governed, and then say of a system that it permits no way for such a modification, except the barbarous and crude way of a sudden and sweeping revolution, have we not in this moment condemned it as a system of a half-civilized social type ?   Yet we are forced to say this, both of the government of the Bourbons and of the more respectable government of democratic Imperialism which reigns in its stead. The only way which the nation has of amending a régime of this sort when it gets out of order, is to rise up and destroy it.   Would an engineer be deemed skilful in his art, if he fortified a place of defence with such strange craft that no breach could be repaired without blowing down the whole wall ?

In the government of advanced societies, like those

of all modern Western States, there is no such thing as stability to be reached, where the majority are gagged and fettered in the conduct of their own public affairs. As by the diffusion and increasing invigoration of civilizing agencies the number of persons in the community with the power of being interested and excited by the business of the community becomes greater and greater, in exactly the same proportion is the danger of autocracy or oligarchy aggravated, and the ground of stability undermined. In the case of an active-minded and political people, military despotism or an artificial oligarchy, whether of a caste or of philosophers or of capitalists, must inevitably rest on hollow and uncertain foundations. Its duration can only depend upon the relation between two things, the mental activity on political matters of the subjects, and the material power of the governors. If the first, under the influence of example in some other nation, or by the pressure of physical wants, waxes heated and aggressive, while the second is weakened in a corresponding measure by disaffection and the difficulty of recruiting it, then the system must fall in a supreme ruin.

Against such a system the French Revolution was, among its other functions, a final denunciation and protest. Its dogma of the Sovereignty of the People—in other words, its claim for the immediate participation of every nation, both in its own internal government and in the choice of attitude to be assumed towards other nations—was levelled against hereditary absolutism, and it will one day be revived against that strange incongruity, democratic despotism. This dogma was exposed, by the way in which it was first propounded, to the attacks both of Burke and of subsequent thinkers. It was based upon that ground of natural, inherent, and imprescriptible right which he and they justly held to be no base at all.[1] To allege that a community had a *right* to govern itself, was necessarily unconvincing to anybody who should choose to allege that a hereditary king or the government of some other community had a right to govern them. Not advancing beyond rights, Filmer and a French Revolutionist were on a par. There was no possibility of any point of reconciliation or common ground between them; so the one flung himself back on Abraham and the Bible, and the other invented a social contract, and then each easily and decisively vanquished the other. If the Revolutionists, instead of reverting to an imaginary social contract which they

[1] Antè, pp. 145-7.

had first to create, had adopted Burke's own standard of the general utility, they could have made out a case for the sovereignty of the people, that for a nation in their then state of mental preparation, would have been thoroughly inexpugnable. If, instead of treading on the narrow and barren metaphysical heights, they had shown that for a highly political people—a people, that is, of great public spirit, great excitability about public affairs, and an ever-increasing capacity of forming judgments upon them—any government in which they do not more or less directly participate is essentially unstable, they would have adduced an argument worth a hundred social contracts. If they had shown, moreover, that certain desirable consequences flow from the government of a people by itself which are wanting in less popular forms—that it increases the stock of national self-respect, a force so strongly protective against petulance, irritable apprehension, and unreasonable jealousy of other nations—that it secures a complete and unwavering regard to the interests of the majority, the first and most difficult of all the ends of government—that it preserves confidence and order by effecting through a peaceful and general expression of popular will those modifications which otherwise can only be achieved by the violent destruction of much that it is desirable to retain—if they had dwelt upon these points, they would have found strong and unshaken arguments for a doctrine, which has only been discredited because it was clothed in flaunting metaphysical garments.

That the criterion of general happiness should have been thus ignored in favour of inherent right, is the more curious, and perhaps the more lamentable, because the Revolution was unquestionably the most gigantic effort that has ever been made to establish this criterion firmly and permanently in political affairs. This task, with a thousand errors of detail, some of them the worst and grossest that the history of politics has to show, with some narrow fanaticism, and with much shortsightedness as to means, the Revolution accomplished. It made conformity to general utility, in its widest sense, the practical standard of the right of any government to the allegiance of its subjects. Thus Burke, the greatest statesman who has adhered to this doctrine, must be pronounced to have been much nearer to the best, most vital, and most durable part of the Revolution than he knew, and than his successors have supposed.

It is not certain that he was not now and then for a moment startled by the suspicion that he might unawares be fighting against the truth. In the midst of flaming and bitter pages, we now and again feel a cool breath from the distant region of a half-pensive tolerance. "I do not think," he says at the close of the *Reflections*, to the person to whom they were addressed, "that my sentiments are likely to alter yours. I do not know that they ought. You are young; you cannot guide, but must follow, the fortune of your country. But hereafter they may be of some use to you, in some future form which your common-wealth may take. In the present it can hardly remain; but before its final settlement, it may be obliged to pass, as one of our poets says, 'through great varieties of untried being,' and in all its transmigrations to be purified by fire and blood."

He felt in the midst of his hate that what he took for seething chaos, might after all be the struggle upwards of the germs of order. Then again, almost the last words he wrote on the Revolution were these :—

"If a great change is to be made in human affairs, the minds of men will be fitted to it; the general opinions and feelings will draw that way. Every fear, every hope will forward it; and then they who persist in opposing this mighty current in human affairs, will appear rather to resist the decrees of Providence itself, than the mere designs of men." With these magnanimous thoughts in his heart, let us leave him. They were the last ray of that *mens divinior* which, amid the sharp press of manifold cares and distractions, had ever vibrated with generous and highminded sympathies, and which, now that the night was falling, did not let go its faith in the beneficent powers and processes of the Unseen Time.

THE END.

LONDON : R. CLAY, SON, AND TAYLOR, PRINTERS.

Check Out More Titles From HardPress Classics Series In this collection we are offering thousands of classic and hard to find books. This series spans a vast array of subjects – so you are bound to find something of interest to enjoy reading and learning about.

Subjects:
Architecture
Art
Biography & Autobiography
Body, Mind &Spirit
Children & Young Adult
Dramas
Education
Fiction
History
Language Arts & Disciplines
Law
Literary Collections
Music
Poetry
Psychology
Science
…and many more.

Visit us at www.hardpress.net

Im TheStory
personalised classic books

"Beautiful gift.. lovely finish.
My Niece loves it, so precious!"

Helen R Brumfielden

⭐⭐⭐⭐⭐

UNIQUE GIFT

FOR KIDS, PARTNERS
AND FRIENDS

Timeless books such as:

Alice in Wonderland · The Jungle Book · The Wonderful Wizard of Oz
Peter and Wendy · Robin Hood · The Prince and The Pauper
The Railway Children · Treasure Island · A Christmas Carol

Romeo and Juliet · Dracula

Visit
Im TheStory.com
and order yours today!

CPSIA information can be obtained
at www.ICGtesting.com
Printed in the USA
BVHW081814220819
556561BV00020B/4685/P